ANGELS ALL AROUND
A Lawyer's Life

Frederick K. Slicker

ISBN: 978-0-9883786-2-9
Published by Yorkshire Publishing, LLC
9731 East 54th Street
Tulsa, OK 74146

DEDICATION

To Laura and Kipp:
May all your days be angelic.

IN HIS PRESENCE

We are standing on holy ground.
And we know there are angels all around.
So let us praise, praise God now.
For we are in His presence on holy ground.

SCRIPTURES

I am sending an angel ahead of you to guard you
along the way and to bring you to the place I have prepared.
Exodus 23:20

If you make the Most High your dwelling
—even the Lord, who is my refuge—
then no harm will befall you,
no disaster will come near your tent.
For he will command his angels concerning you
to guard you in all your ways.
Psalm 91:9-12

A Word About Angels

Angels have appeared throughout history in classical literature and in the sacred texts of Christianity, Judaism, Islam, Hinduism, Buddhism and other major religions. Angels are messengers from God invested by God with divine powers to help, to protect and to guard. They hover between heaven and earth, waiting to be sent by God to intervene in the lives of men. There are armies of angels and personal angels. There are guardian angels and avenging angels. There are good angels and evil angels.

Angels are typically depicted as beautiful spirits, heavenly beings, ethereal shapes reflecting God's hope, peace, grace and joy. Angels always have wings, sometimes halos and usually long flowing gowns. Angels often carry musical instruments. They sound the trumpets, ring the bells and proclaim in music God's glory.

Angels appeared to Jesus throughout his life. An angel spoke to Mary, informing her that she was pregnant with God's only Son. Angels announced the birth of a new born King and became a symphony of heavenly hosts whose voices praised God. An angel appeared in the tomb, telling the disciples that Jesus had risen. Angels bring messages from God to man in very special ways.

I had never really thought much about angels prior to reading Frank Peretti's *This Present Darkness*, a story of a cosmic collision between a young professor's guardian angels and avenging angels determined to spread evil in their wake. The angels in *This Present Darkness* became real, vivid and scary.

Images of angels typically show very young girls with wings and depict a statue of beauty, flying through the air, seeking to spread God's blessings. Rarely do we see a picture of an angel that is alive, real and available.

This is the story of how my angel became a real, ever-present spirit of God's constant reminder that I am a child of the Most High God, blessed to be a blessing to others, protected by His grace and surrounded by His love. Some will doubt the existence of my angel. Others may dispute my interpretation of the role played by my angel. What I believe is this: Only an angel sent from God could explain all the many blessings and all the many miracles that I have experienced and continue to enjoy. Thanks Be To God!

INTRODUCTION

May 1999 was a very big month for the Slicker family. Laura graduated from Emory Law School in Atlanta with a Juris Doctor. Kipp graduated from Boston College with a Bachelor of Arts with honors. Laura got married to Harvey Lucas Mayes, IV, a law school classmate from Powder Springs, GA. The wedding was awesome, the best wedding I have ever attended. So much joy, so much happiness! I am a man truly blessed beyond belief.

I wanted to give Laura and Kipp something very special for their graduation gift. I decided to collect stories from my past and share them with Laura and Kipp, so that they might know me better. They know I am a lawyer, but they do not know what I actually do as a lawyer. This book is my attempt to file that void. I have emphasized my practice of law and the unusual, diverse and most interesting aspects of what has occurred in my practice. I have intentionally omitted discussion of all the many defining moments of their lives, since those moments are their stories, not mine.

This book is an effort to illustrate how God's angels have helped me at crucial times in my life and how those same angels have been with me and guided me as a lawyer under all kinds of situations and circumstances.

To write a book about the past, I had to try to remember what happened, why it happened and when it happened. I am quite sure that I have made some errors in reporting the past. If so, they are unintentional but totally my fault and my responsibility. I take full credit and full responsibility for the mistakes contained in these materials.

I apologize in advance if I have incorrectly attributed a statement, a fact or an event to the wrong person. Please forgive me.

I discovered that the following truths are what is important:

1. There is a holy God.
2. He is alive, active, personal and available.
3. He is all knowing, all powerful, always present, always available.
4. He is in me, for me and with me for all good purposes.
5. Where I am, He is there also, so I am perpetually in His Presence.
6. He is in control.
7. I can trust Him completely.
8. His angels are all around me, guiding and protecting me.

TO GOD BE THE GLORY. AMEN AND AMEN.

PREFACE

I have been a Boy Scout, a student, a soldier, a lawyer, a judge, a husband, a father and a man. I have tried to do what is right. I have sometimes succeeded, sometimes failed, sometimes just survived. I have tried to be a problem solver, a listener, a helper, a supporter, a friend, someone who reduces tensions and looks for the good in people. I have made some footprints in the sand along the way. There have been victories and defeats, highs and lows, peaks and valleys, joys and heartaches. I have dreamed dreams, seen visions, set goals, earned awards, received honors, been embarrassed, acted stupidly, chosen badly and on occasion even acted wisely.

I have tried to be the best father possible. Laura and Kipp know that they are and will always be loved by me unconditionally, under all circumstances, no matter what.

This is my story, what little I remember of it. These are my defining moments, the memories of what shaped me and molded me into who I am as a lawyer and who I am becoming as a father and as a man. Life is a journey, a series of experiences lived, a collection of choices made, paths followed, mistakes endured, challenges met and victories won. In every moment, there is a chance to choose, a victory to win, a defeat to avoid, an opportunity to seize. My short-falls, my anxieties, my joys, my enthusiasm, my excitement, my search for success and my reach for what is my call have left me with some insights worthy of repeating.

There has been constant tension in my life between what I should do when facing various important alternatives and conflicting key values. The honorable life is not just a Sunday-kind-of-life, but it is a daily moment-by-moment experience. Choosing what to do is important each moment, deciding what is most important now, anticipating future moments and seeking a balance among important priorities continue. This balancing act is called life. *Carpe diem!*

This book is not intended to dramatize my life into something more than it is. Rather, my purpose is to summarize my experiences as a lawyer, so that Laura and Kipp and others will better understand me and learn lessons from my experiences. For the sins and successes of their father will shape their thoughts, their attitudes, their actions, their reactions, their hopes, their dreams, their aspirations, their visions and their future. At the same time, my story continues.

The Early Years
1943-1956

I have no recollection of the small apartment in the Kendall Whittier area near the University of Tulsa, my first home. My earliest recollections relate to our small frame house at 735 North Florence Place in North Tulsa. We had two large trees in the front yard to climb. I frequently fell out of both. We had a garden with asparagus, onions, radishes and tomatoes in the back. No matter what you do, once asparagus gets established, like kudzu and bamboo, it is almost impossible to kill, which is what as a young boy I wanted to do, since I hated the taste of asparagus. Now I crave it as a special delicacy. The garden was shaded by a wonderful cherry tree, which I still recall each time I enjoy cherry pie.

We enjoyed a large screened-in back porch that ran most of the entire length of the back of the house. The porch was on the east side, and it provided the only place to get relief from the blazing summer sun. There was no such thing as air conditioning in those days, so we stripped to our shorts and simply endured the summer heat. Was it ever hot!

The backyard provided Phil, my older brother, and Richard, my younger brother, and me with a place to play baseball, which dominated my early days. The yard was too small to have a whole field, so we put home plate in one corner. After we hit the ragged old ball with our stick bats, we ran the wrong direction to third base. If we got to third, then we ran backwards to second and then home. Our objective was to get home safely. Running backwards around the bases would later prove embarrassing to Phil, when more than ten years later, Phil drove a frozen rope deep into left field at Will Rogers High School. Unbelievably, Phil ran to third base, instead of to first base. He had an impossible task explaining to his coaches and teammates what the hell he was thinking. I knew that he was simply lost in the ecstasy and revere of memories from our early years.

We always had a ball game going with the neighbors or just among the three of us. These were fierce contests of will and dexterity, often involving most of the neighborhood. The four Lucas boys later starred in basketball at Will Rogers High School, the University of Tulsa and Oral Roberts University. Jim Wixon, another neighbor, was older but part of the neighborhood team. He is still the only player to have pitched a no-hitter in the College World Series at Omaha, NE. He played for Oklahoma A & M, later to become OSU. These neighborhood kids were good athletes who learned to compete, at least in part, in our backyard.

When we were not playing baseball, we played endless games of Cowboys and Indians. We created rubber band guns from old inner tubes, and we made match guns that shot stick matches. One fine day, I almost burned down a neighbor's garage when a grass fire started from a stick match shot from my clothespin match gun. Life was a little hot around the hood for me after that, with no one getting to touch match guns ever again.

In one game of Cowboys and Indians, I got so mad at Richard that I shot a home made arrow from my homemade bow at him as he was running to get away. Fortunately, I was a lousy shot, since the arrow went between his legs, causing him to trip. He broke the arrow, and I spent the next three nights alone in my bedroom with no dessert, thinking about what could have happened had I actually hit him. That was the last arrow I ever shot at anyone.

We had no television in those days. We did have a radio, which we wore out listening to *The Shadow*, *The Lone Ranger* and Cardinal baseball with Harry Cary calling play-by-play for the games. When

I was nine, we got a fat roly-poly dog we named "Rinty," after Rin Tin Tin. Rinty was part golden retriever, part lab and part Heinz 57 variety. He lived to be almost twenty. He was great fun and a great companion.

The rest of our entertainment consisted of going to my baseball games or my brothers' games or Tulsa Oiler games. We always sat in the right field bleachers at the Oiler games, which were separated from the main stadium seats by a chain link fence. We took our gloves in order to catch a foul ball, knowing that the chances of that were pretty small. Dad was always there with us. We would get to share a ten cent Coke and a five cent bag of popcorn, while watching the wannabe minor leaguers play some terrific baseball. Sometimes, Mom would drop us off at the ball park two hours before game time, so that we could wait for batting practice home runs that sailed out of the park. There were many scuffles with other kids for these balls, but Phil was big, and he usually captured the prize. Those Oiler batting practice balls were put to good use and were completely worn out by our endless games at home. Several years later, I would get to watch Phil and Richard play on the same Oiler ball diamond. What a thrill!

We got our first black and white TV when I was in the fourth grade. Before that, the only time we were able to watch TV was at the Westoffs' home for Wednesday night fights and New Year's Day college football bowl games. Dad would get to enjoy a cold beer on those occasions, but Dad would share his beer with each of us getting a sip, so that there was very little left when Dad got the can back. I never really liked beer, but there was no way that I would admit that in front of my brothers or my Dad.

I remember trips to Wichita and McPherson, KS, at Easter and Christmas. Phil was the oldest of what would become twenty-three Nordling grandchildren on mother's side of the family. I was the second oldest. Mother was the second oldest of two sisters and three brothers. Chester, Bernard, and Lee served in WWII, and later became prominent lawyers in Western Kansas. Mother's older sister, Verna, died of cancer at the age forty. Her younger sister, Dorothy, died in 1991 after several months of pain following a traffic accident at 57th and Sheridan in Tulsa.

It was always a joy to go to Grandma Nordling's home in McPherson. She had a wonderful vegetable and flower garden in her backyard. There were always delicious smells coming from her kitchen. When the three Slicker boys showed up in McPherson, hot cinnamon rolls were waiting, but they were not there long. We could eat a couple dozen rolls before taking a breath.

Grandpa Nordling was a huge man. He had once been the Sheriff of McPherson County. He had huge hands. If a stern glance did not produce the proper corrective action, I did not need a spanking, just the touch of his huge hand on my shoulder was enough to correct my wayward thoughts or actions. I remember going fishing with Grandpa in the park in McPherson. He was a good fisherman and a wonderful storyteller. He was a gentle giant, and I loved to be in his presence and share his company.

The Nordling family in McPherson celebrated their Swedish heritage each Christmas. Potato sausage, rye bread, lukfisk and gravy, buttery spreetz and other wonderful food was routine. All six Nordling children and all twenty-three Nordling grandchildren gathered for Christmas Eve every year. The presents under the tree literally filled the Nordling living room. Christmas Eve dinner was a traditional Swedish feast beyond our wildest dreams. Santa Claus would come around 7:30 p.m. and give one present to each person. We would go to bed filled with excitement. On Christmas morning, we would go as a family to the traditional Swedish Yulota Christmas sunrise service at 5:00 a.m. at the local Lutheran church. After church, everyone returned to the Nordling's home to open gifts. Christmas was awesome and joyous at the Nordling's, as it should be.

Easter was also lots of fun. We would color Easter eggs on Saturday and hide literally dozens of eggs in the Nordling's lush green lawn. These were real eggs, not the hollow plastic kind used today. Deviled eggs are a favorite of mine, partly because the colored eggs not thrown at my brothers Easter morning would be deviled to eat after church. We always went as a family to the sunrise service on Easter morning.

The Slicker family in Wichita was older. Grandma and Grandpa Slicker worked hard. They welcomed us into their home, but there was not much excitement. Dad was an exception. He was a prankster and kidder. The Slickers always had great food to eat and lots of chocolate candy. Dad's sister, Marie, was rarely there, and his brother, Howard, suffered from tuberculosis and lived in Arizona. Aunt LaRue lived at 402 North Rutan in Wichita with her parents. She worked for more than fifty years in the engineering department of the City of Wichita before she retired to the Presbyterian Manor, where she celebrated her 100th birthday shortly before her death.

Religious training was not part of the public school curriculum, but every Wednesday Sequoyah Elementary School was adjourned early, so that all the children could walk to a nearby Baptist church for Bible training. This practice occurred about the time the United States Supreme Court first ruled that government written, officially sanctioned prayers recited in public schools were unconstitutional.

Many in the evangelical Christian community today cite that decision as the beginning of the moral decay in the United States. I believe the Court was absolutely correct in that case. Government is supposed to be neutral when it comes to religion, not the official sponsor of any particular beliefs. Current religious leaders ignore the history that gave rise to the founding of America. It was the desire for free expression of religious beliefs, unfettered by government compulsion or interference, that fueled the founding fathers to leave Europe and settle in America, that populated early pre-revolutionary America and that breathed life into what was a major force in the American dream. Many of our spiritual leaders today fail to recall that governmental interference with religious beliefs and practices has devastated the development of man's journey on earth. Parents, not public schools or government bureaucrats, should teach children about religion and religious fundamentals.

For public schools to exclude God and all references to the religious history of the times is equally, if not more, objectionable. The history of Western Europe could not be told without referring to the religious events that dominated its entire history. In my view, religious history should be a mandatory class in the history department of every school, public and private. It should not be presented to the students in science class.

In the 1950s, I was too young to know of Hitler or of the Nazi efforts to exterminate the Jews. I was too young to know about Hiroshima and Nagasaki, but I felt the fear, anxiety and genuine concern that exploding the atomic bomb had in my early years. Many of our friends and neighbors built bomb shelters in their back yards to survive the first blast of the next war. I was also too young to understand the threat of Communism, the expansion of the USSR, the beginnings of the Cold War, the fear of China and North Korea or the threat of polio. I only knew tranquility, baseball, scouting and church.

I recall the special interest taken in me by some of my elementary school teachers, especially Mrs. Gordon in the fourth grade and Mrs. Harper in the sixth grade. I remember Mrs. Harper asking me if I knew Braille. Apparently, I pressed so hard on my pencil that indentions were made in the paper. I did not even know what Braille was, so her joke was lost on me.

I remember only a few of the kids from Sequoyah. I remember David Curnutt, who would later be president of my Edison High School Sophomore Class (I was vice president). There was Tanya West, who was the daughter of Woody West, the basketball coach at Will Rogers High School. She would later marry James "Country" King, an All-America basketball player at TU and an NBA star. They would become my friends at First Methodist Church. There was

Dick Goodson and Larry Wilson, my best friends from scouting, and Scottie Jacobs, whose father coached the Sequoyah Indians, my first baseball team.

All in all, my elementary school days were spent in relative tranquility. I learned some basics and knew I had an aptitude for math. I tried hard, I was encouraged by my teachers and I was passed along each year. I learned to read some, but I also detested reading, especially when I was asked to read out loud in front of the class. I usually screwed up, felt embarrassed and heard the snickers of my friends. Reading out loud demonstrated my lack of reading proficiency. I hated it.

I was a member of the Tulsa Boys Singers when I was eleven. I had an average voice, but I loved to sing. I recall rehearsals at the University of Tulsa. One day I was supposed to walk home after rehearsal. Unfortunately, I went the wrong way and ended up lost on 11th Street, totally confused and frightened. My house was seven blocks north of Admiral, not eleven blocks south of Admiral. To this day, I really get apprehensive, even sometimes scared, when I do not know where I am.

I remember taking trombone lessons at Central High School in downtown Tulsa. The Central High building housed a basement gym where as a high school sophomore I would play basketball. The end of the court was adjacent to a brick wall, so when you drove to the basket for a lay up, you crashed into the brick wall. Central High's varsity team was then coached by Eddie Sutton, the legendary Hall of Fame college basketball coach. The building has been totally remodeled and now houses AEP/Public Service Company of Oklahoma's headquarters.

One day following our music lessons, my brother Phil and I got into some kind of argument, so instead of waiting for Mom to pick us up, I decided to walk home with my trombone in hand. I always had a stubborn streak, which persists even to today. From Central High School in downtown Tulsa to our home in Northeast Tulsa was at least a five mile walk. Despite the heat, I made it home safely. Mom was furious, Phil was vindicated and I was punished (as was appropriate).

Mowing lawns was an important early experience for me. I started mowing lawns when I was eleven. I used a push mower, hand clippers and hand shears initially, because we did not have a power mower or trimmers. The work was hot and very hard. I thought I was in heaven when Dad brought home our first power mower. I could mow one or two lawns a day, make some money early in the mornings and still have time to play baseball in the afternoon. Mowing lawns taught me first hand that "a job is not worth doing unless you do your best."

From mowing lawns, I had a little money that I could bank. I carefully kept records of my income and saved all I could for college. I paid most of the tuition and board and room for my first two undergraduate years at KU out of my lawn mowing money. Those funds enabled me to make the extra $56 payment per semester for out of state tuition at Kansas University, over and above the $205 per semester for in-state tuition at KU.

Dad always inspected the lawns I mowed. If the lawn did not pass his inspection, I went back to do it again until it was right. I learned to take pride in my work and not to disappoint Dad. If the work I did was not worth my pride, then it was not worth my effort. It always takes longer to do my best. Through Dad's example, I learned that if you do not have time to do the task right the first time, when will you have time to correct it later?

I recall mowing Cap Lamb's lawn. Cap was the elderly band director at Cleveland Junior High School. He had played the trombone in John Phillip Sousa's marching band when he was younger. After two years of mowing his lawn, Cap gave me his old trombone. With my mowing money, I bought a new trombone that carried me through my sophomore year in high school, when I played in the Edison marching band. Cap Lamb was a friend and always an encourager.

For two years every Saturday morning from age eleven until I was thirteen, I attended confirmation classes at First Lutheran Church at 13th and Utica. I memorized the Ten Commandments, the Apostles' and Nicene Creeds and a variety of scriptural passages. I was confirmed with eight others on Pentecost Sunday in May 1956. John Running, later an All State halfback in my 1961 Edison High School graduating class, was in my catechism class, as was my cousin, Kent Sloan, both of whom later became lawyers. Andrea Nielson, the daughter of Dorothy Nielson, was also in our class.

Boy Scouts provided me many memorable adventures and numerous memories. Dad was always there. He was Scout master, assistant Scout master and father to many of the boys in the troop. He never missed a camp out. What was very clear, very comforting and sometimes annoying was my sure knowledge that he would be there, watching but not inhibiting my experience. If I needed him, he was there. It was comforting, since I always knew that I could depend on him if I had a problem, which usually occurred because I failed to bring matches or toilet paper. I knew that going snipe hunting or going on a panty raid at the nearby Girl Scout camps or smoking grapevines was not an option for me. My participating in those activities would have hurt and disappointed my father. Dad was a great man who loved his boys. In deciding whether to take an action, even in my adult life, many times I have asked, "Would Dad approve?" I knew that I should not do it if the answer was no or unclear.

Boy Scouts provided many opportunities to walk. I hiked several times to Mohawk Park to fish in the lake there. I even walked to 51st and South Yale to fish in the LaFortune Park pond. Today, it would not be wise for a parent to let his children walk all over town, but then it seemed the natural thing to do.

It rained or snowed on almost every scout camping trip I took. The weather was either very cold or unbearably hot, and we always got thoroughly filthy and wet. Most of my campouts were at Camp Garland near Grove, OK. Parts of the campgrounds were new, recently cleared and sometimes truly dangerous. I vividly remember the time I woke up in my two man wall tent at 3:00 a.m. one cold October morning with a large copper head snake curled up in the middle of the tent. Had I stepped off the cot, I might have died, since copperheads are extremely poisonous. I screamed, and Dad came running. He located a long wooden tent poll and hammered that copper head into kingdom come. Among the other scouts, I was a hero, since the snake chose my tent, but I was scared until I realized that Dad was there to protect me.

I was the Senior Patrol Leader on one camp out. After helping the younger scouts pitch their tents and campfires, Larry Smith and I found a nice soft area to pitch our tent. The rest of the campsite had sharp flint stones everywhere. We built an enormous fire, the best one ever, and settled in for the night around 9:30 p.m. It was really dark; the only light was from the harvest moon and stars that were covered by clouds that night and the glowing embers of a great fire mostly burned out. Then it rained, a torrential rain, three to four inches in an hour. At 3:30 a.m., everything in our tent was washed outside. The fire had caved in the metal plate that covered a twelve foot deep sinkhole, and we were sopping wet. All the younger scouts laughed. After a while, we laughed too. Sometimes experience produces unwarranted confidence. Taking the soft, easy way usually results in disaster. Our campsite was soft, because of its location at the bottom of the gully. I should have known better, but I did not look around carefully enough.

One early defining moment was my Eagle Scout Court of Honor. Glenn Dobbs, the All American football player and Tulsa University head football coach, spoke. I was thirteen. I actually finished the Eagle requirements in July, before my thirteenth birthday, but there was no Court of Honor during August or September. I think I was the youngest Eagle Scout in Troop 37, perhaps the youngest Eagle Scout in any Oklahoma troop. It gave me great joy to pin the little Eagle Scout pin on Mom's jacket. This achievement required earning at least twenty one merit badges. It took two years of focused effort and lots of hard work. I could not have earned my Eagle without Mom and Dad assisting me.

Phil and I received the Lutheran God and Country *"Pro deo et patrae"* award, the third and fourth Boy Scouts in Oklahoma to receive this award. One requirement was to give at least 150 hours of service to our church. Neither the Eagle Scout award nor the God and Country Award would have been possible had not Mom and Dad been there to support and encourage us. Had Dad not been there helping us mow and trim the church lawn, we would never have accumulated 150 hours of service, but Dad was there to help. He was always encouraging, never compelling, never demanding. He should have received the award for the *Greatest Dad.* He more than earned it, but he never took credit or desired recognition. It was more than enough for him to watch his sons being honored.

I attended Cleveland Junior High School in the seventh grade. I remember attending wood and metal shop classes where, for the first time, I got to make something with my hands. Fortunately, this taught me to try something else, since I was not very good at hand work. One day, while we were waiting for our teacher to arrive and begin our class, I said, "Speak of the devil," when he approached. I meant no disrespect. This was just an expression that I had heard recently. But he did not take the comment kindly. I was required to duck walk around the class for the entire next hour. I almost passed out. Had I not been a catcher with strong legs, I would not have been able to finish that class. Had my parents known about this incident, they would probably have applauded the teacher's willingness to take a special interest in me by disciplining their errant son's mis-conduct and stupid comment.

I remember two other events that were not very pleasant. The boy's name was Jimmy Reed. He was smaller than I was, but he was a tough kid. He was also a real wise ass and bully. One day he was picking on another student. I attempted to intervene on behalf of the other student, trying to be helpful to my classmate. Jimmy Reed took my interference as a challenge to his manhood. A confrontation was scheduled the next day at 8:00 a.m. in front of the school for all our classmates to observe.

I had never been in a fight before, and I had never intended to provoke a fight this time, but events led me to accept his challenge. Boy, was that a mistake! I thought I had to fight to protect my honor. I also thought that I would whoop his ass, since I was bigger than he was. The fight only lasted two minutes before the principal broke it up. Instead of me winning, Jimmy Reed kicked my ass. Even worse, he wore rings on his fingers that drew blood and marked my face. I could not even hide the marks or the embarrassment from losing to that little punk. I learned then that emotional talk provokes emotional reactions. I also learned that being small in stature does not make one small in action. I was a lousy fighter, so if I was going to fight, I had better learn how to win.

Two weeks later, a seventh and eighth grade wrestling tournament was announced. I signed up. Unfortunately for me, my first opponent was an experienced eighth grader. I was a skinny seventh grade kid with no experience. This supervised fight lasted maybe forty-five seconds before I got pinned. I got my ass kicked again. I was extremely glad that in March 1956, my parents bought a house at 41st and Pittsburgh in the Edison High School district in South Tulsa. I would not be returning to Cleveland for the eighth grade. Had I done so, I might not have survived another year, especially given my lack of fighting proficiency.

Edison
1956-1961

I tried out for a summer baseball team in the Edison district in the spring of 1956. I had never been a star, but I had always started on my team at Sequoyah, and I had been a solid player. I tried out for a team coached by Mr. Dunbar, the same coach and the same team my Sequoyah Indians defeated in the fourth grade city semi-final championship game. The Eisenhower team was heavily favored, but we were one run ahead in the top of the fifth inning in a five-inning game. Eisenhower was a really good team, well coached, disciplined and talented. My Sequoyah Indians were also a pretty good team. Early in the game, I drove in the potential winning run with a double. As I rounded first base, Pete White, a huge fourth grader, tripped me as I rounded first. When I got up, I was thrown out at second base. No interference call was made, but the run counted, since the runner had crossed home before I was tagged out at second for the third out.

With one out and runners at first and third in the top of the fifth inning, Eisenhower tried a suicide squeeze play. I was catching. I had never even heard of a squeeze play. I did not know about catcher's interference. I simply saw the runner coming home from third base. I stepped out in front of the plate, caught the ball and tagged the runner out. The batter, instead of swinging his bat, stepped out of the batter's box. All the batter had to do was touch me with his bat, and he would have been on first base with the bases loaded. All hell broke loose. The Eisenhower coaches, players and parents were screaming and ran out all over the field. Fortunately, the umpire called the play correctly. The runner was out, the pitch was a strike, the game was over, and we were on our way to the city championship game. Unfortunately, we lost the final game the next night.

What really sealed my baseball fate was that I had three problems. While I was a really good catcher, I could not hit my way out of a paper bag. I had a very weak arm, and I ran too long in one place. In short, I was not very good, despite my desire and my hard work. If you cannot hit, throw or run, you have little future in baseball, no matter how much desire you have or how hard you work at it.

I wanted to play baseball so badly I could taste it. I wanted to get better, play with a very competitive team and go on to play baseball professionally. While I made the Eisenhower team, I did not play at all that summer. I caught in the bullpen, warmed up pitchers, shagged fly balls, carried all the equipment, cheered the team and warmed the bench. I was a decent cheerleader but a discouraged ballplayer. I was devastated after each game. Even when we were winning big and the score was totally lopsided, I did not get to play at all. I thought then that this was punishment for that game in the fourth grade. Maybe it was.

I was not as good as those who were playing ahead of me. Doug Martin, later an All State catcher at Edison and a three year letterman at OU, was catching in front of me. He was a terrific athlete, an excellent hitter with a strong accurate arm. He was both fast and quick and a talented catcher. But I was not so bad as to not play at all.

I began to wear glasses shortly after that summer, and wearing glasses was a major detriment for a catcher. Sweat often dripped onto my glasses and blurred my vision. Nevertheless, I wanted to catch. I was a good catcher. I was stubborn. I should have tried another position, but I liked to catch, because the catcher controls the game. Behind home plate was where the game was centered. Other positions were boring by comparison. I learned by this experience not to be so rigid in what I wanted. I learned to be more flexible, a quality which has characterized my legal career. I am willing to work on a project that is out of the box and out of my comfort zone. I do not have to work only on specific matters within a specific specialty.

Edison Junior High School was a very different place from Cleveland. During my first semester at Edison, the high school was still under construction. Consequently, seventh and eighth grade students went to school from 7:00 a.m. until 12:20 p.m. Senior high school students went from 1:30 p.m. to 5:00 p.m. This left the afternoons open for study for the younger students, and study I did. I was assigned to a ninth grade math class, even though my Cleveland seventh grade math class had not finished the basic seventh grade materials, and I had studied none of the eighth grade materials. I literally had to study math four or five hours a day just to make C's, which I did the first semester. This was a defining moment for me. Learning required hard work. Study was not simple. C's were not acceptable. I got a B second semester, but the first semester C was probably the most important grade I ever got before college.

Angels were there to help me simply pass math in the eighth grade, even though I worked harder than I had ever worked before. Moving from a C to a B in that class taught me that I could improve if I focused, committed and worked hard. This was a lesson I would re-learn several times later in my school and professional life. Refusing to be an average C student forced me to work hard, especially since I was not as smart as many of the others in my class. I liked Edison Junior High School a lot. I was challenged, and the students were really friendly. For the first time in my school life, I felt like I was home.

I was not a good high school athlete, but I played sophomore basketball and sophomore and junior baseball. Basketball was an enormous amount of work for me. I was probably the thirteenth man on a fifteen man all-sophomore roster. I ran stairs, worked out on weights and ran the court in "suicide" drills. Mostly, I was used as cannon fodder for the better players. I did play a little, and I was even high point man for our team in my last game. We were getting beat by the Booker T. Washington's sophomore team by at least thirty points. I got to play about four minutes in the fourth quarter. I made five points and sank all of the shots I tried. The next Monday I got cut from the team along with six other players. My high school basketball career was over.

About two weeks before that last game, I was guarding the number one sophomore guard. He faked one way, and I went that way. He drove around me the other way, sinking an easy lay up. Coach Grove blew his whistle and came onto the court with a strange inquisitive look on his face as he looked at the ceiling. After what seemed like an eternity, but was probably only a few seconds, he asked me if that was my jock up there in the rafters. Everyone laughed but me. In hindsight, it was really pretty funny, but not to me at the time. I was kept on the team, because I worked my ass off. No one worked harder than I did. I simply was not very quick, not very fast and not very good. I found running difficult. I was a lousy shooter. When I jumped my total vertical leap was only a few inches. I never even touched the rim. I had a sense of where I ought to be, but I had a hard time getting there. I concluded I would be better in a more measured, more precise game: baseball.

I was a pretty good baseball player. I was one of only a few sophomores that made the varsity high school team. My only problem was that I was a catcher, and my older brother, Phil, was the senior catcher at the time. Phil was a great high school baseball player. In one game at Will Rogers High School, I saw Phil hit a ball harder than any ball I have ever seen hit. It was a laser shot over the left fielder's head. The ball never got more than fifteen feet off the ground, but the left fielder still had not gotten to the ball when Phil crossed home plate. He was a terrific hitter. Phil was the first All State baseball player at Edison. It was a joy for me to catch behind him, because I learned so much from him and because I thought

16

my time would come when he graduated. I did get to warm up Jack Spurgin and Gary Lewis, the two sophomore pitchers stars.

In my junior year, the senior football quarterback was recruited to be the catcher. I thought I had earned the starting catcher position because of all my work as a sophomore. I should have known better, but I thought my time would come as a junior. I learned again that desire and hard work are good but not good enough. Talent counts. So I continued to catch the bullpen, work harder than anyone else and basically not play as a junior.

Just before baseball practice started my senior year in January 1961, Doug Martin transferred to Edison. He was a three sport letterman in football, baseball and basketball at Webster and a gifted catcher and hitter. He transferred to Edison so that he could catch Jack Spurgin and Gary Lewis in their final high school year before they were drafted and played the next five years in AAA professional baseball. I was really hurt, but he was so much better than I was. Even though I was almost elected captain of the team (I lost by one vote), I decided to hang up my cleats. The team went on to win the Oklahoma state high school championship. Gary Lewis, Jack Spurgin and Doug Martin were selected All State. Gary and Jack signed professional contracts, and Doug signed to play at OU, where he was the starting catcher his last three years there. He never played professionally to my knowledge, though he was a graduate student coach at OU for at least one year after he stopped playing. Doug is now a mortician. Gary is an international tax lawyer. I have lost track of Jack.

When I left the team, I planned to participate in the Kiwanis International oratory contest. In truth, leaving my high school baseball team was one of the few times in my life when I feel like I quit. I have regretted leaving the team ever since. Had I stayed, I would not have played, but I would have been part of a state championship baseball team. I could have been a bullpen catcher and a team cheerleader as the team went on to win the state championship. So much for high school sports!

High school was a time of great excitement in a variety of ways for me that did not involve sports. There were three musical class plays, one each year, in which I was a singer and dancer. I did not have a speaking part in the plays. I enjoyed the singing and dancing, though I was a lousy singer and clumsy dancer. These class plays took an enormous amount of time, but I really had fun participating.

I was elected to Key Club as a sophomore. This was a real honor. Only ten boys out of my class of 765 students were elected. I was appointed Texas-Oklahoma District Treasurer under the governorship of Van Smithen of Tulsa Edison. Kent McCoin, a Key Clubber from North Dallas, preceded me in that office. As a senior, I was elected Lt. Governor of the Northeastern Oklahoma Division, which included Bartlesville. My Key Club experience included two district meetings, one in Dallas and one in Waco, Texas, as well as one international convention in Toronto, Canada. Our group from the Texas-Oklahoma District traveled by train from Tulsa to Dallas to New Orleans, then north through Washington DC, New York City and Niagara Falls to Toronto. We arrived in Toronto shortly after the opening of the St. Lawrence Seaway, so the city of Toronto was decked out in flags of many nations. This was a tremendous experience.

I was an active participant in student government, where I served as vice president of both my sophomore and junior classes and as a member of the student council all three years in high school. Student government involved a variety of activities. I ran for senior class president and President of Key Club, but I was defeated by Don Patterson. Don was captain of the basketball team, an All City basketball player, an excellent student and a very popular leader of our class. He did a great job as President of both Key Club and the Class of 1961.

I recall several fun events that occurred during high school. Jack Dobblebower was my advanced math teacher. He was a lot of fun and a terrific teacher. He kept a pet alligator in his classroom, a gift from a former class. He had a gossip/suggestion box in his class. He knew who was dating whom, who had broken up with whom and what the latest gossip was about everyone in the class. He was a gifted teacher and a tremendously positive influence on many students at Edison, including me. I was able to quiz out of five hours of college calculus and major in math at KU, largely because of his influence and support.

Mr. Dobblebower was called to the office one day. Someone suggested that we pile our shoes on his desk. When he returned, he announced we had three minutes to get all of our shoes off his desk and on the right feet or we would have a test on the material he was going to teach the next day. We scrambled to comply. Of course we did not make it. We took the test, which I aced, but most of the other people in the class did not. It was great fun.

When I was a senior, Mr. Dobblebower's classroom was moved to a prefabricated frame building behind the permanent high school building. We were too loud to remain in the main building. Mr. Dobblebower's classroom had a cloakroom that was separated from the adjoining classroom. My classmates were really smart. One of the guys put an old toilet in the cloakroom. When Mr.Dobblebower opened the door, there was a flushing sound and one of the girls in the class screamed as she got up from the unattached fake toilet. Unfortunately, the flushing sound went over the entire school intercom system. Mr. Dobblebower laughed hysterically, and then when he was disciplined for his unruly class, we were punished with an extra series of tests. There was minor hell to pay, but it was hilarious.

Mrs. Blythe, a librarian by trade, had taken two classes in physics in college, so she was technically qualified to teach the senior physics class. She was out of her league in physics, and all of the seniors knew it, especially those from Jack Dobblebower's advanced math class. As a result, we played lots of tricks on her, both before and during her class. Most of the formulas which are used in basic physics were developed from Calculus I or Calculus II. Since the seniors came from Mr. Dobblebower's advanced calculus class directly into her class, many times we had developed those formulas in math, and many times she rarely knew the material well enough to teach it.

Her class was in a chemistry lab that had long tables instead of desks for the students. One day, Charles Bott, my tablemate, took a dime and unscrewed all of the screws in the bottom of the table. When Mrs. Blythe came into the room, he stood up and acted like he was leaning on the table, but he put no weight on it. When Mrs. Blythe came up to talk to him, she leaned on the table; and the whole table collapsed. Everybody in the room thought it was absolutely hilarious, except Mrs. Blythe. Fortunately, no one was hurt, except for Mrs. Blythe's feelings.

Charlie put a large can of marbles on Mrs. Blythe's desk, but before he did, he cut out the bottom and added a little oil. When she picked up the can, greasy marbles went all over everywhere. It was almost impossible to pick up those damn marbles. We thought it was hilarious. Mrs. Blythe was not amused. Charlie is now a Lutheran minister in Billings, Montana.

We had sock hops after every football and basketball game, mixers after most wrestling and swimming meets. We had at least one school sponsored dance every month. Many of the guys and girls joined "social clubs," which were groups organized primarily for partying, smoking and holding monthly dances. Boys and girls dated when I was in high school, unlike today where boys and girls "go out" as a group but not with an individual.

In February 1961, I began dating Betty Broding. She was a devout Catholic, incredibly bright and deeply spiritual. She is one of the smartest people I have ever known. We had long conversations about the difference between Catholics and Protestants, the influence of the Pope, about the celibacy of priests and nuns, the number and meaning of the sacraments, the "priesthood of all believers," salvation through faith alone, Martin Luther's 95 Theses and a variety of other religious topics. Her depth of knowledge and sensitivity in spiritual matters was incredible, especially since she was only eighteen at the time.

Betty was voted most likely to succeed out of our class of 765. She attended Rice University on a full scholarship. She has a PhD in organic chemistry and advanced degrees in biology and physics. She recently retired from teaching organic chemistry at the University of Southern California as a full professor, where she frequently won "Best Teacher" awards. She continues to write poetry. Betty had dated Bill Goodwin for most of her senior year. Bill had asked her to the senior prom, and she had accepted months before. Betty and Bill went to the senior prom together, so I needed a date to the prom.

I began dating Linda Morgan in mid-May, after Betty and Bill got back together. I took Linda to the prom. I had admired her for a long time and even tried to date her the year earlier, but Linda had always dated older guys, even if they were in college. She was a real lady, lots of fun and always happy. I was serious and very naïve. We saw each other almost every evening during the summer of 1961 before she went to OU and I went to KU. Absence makes the heart wander, not grow fonder. I thought that if she loved me, she would come to KU, though I never asked her to do so. We saw each other at Christmas and at 1962 Spring break and dated throughout the Summer of 1962. During one of our conversations, I mentioned that I was considering going into the ministry. She could not see herself as a minister's wife. Ironically, I would have been a lousy minister had I received a call into the ministry, but she would have been the perfect minister's wife.

We broke up after our third semester of college, when Linda came home at Christmas with a fraternity lavaliere given to her by her future husband. Linda graduated from OU with an elementary education degree in art. She married soon after graduation. She has two adult children and two granddaughters. She lives in Boerne, Texas, with her second husband. She was always fun, always smiling, always a lady and always treated me special.

Ken Burton, one of my best friends, had a car. We double dated at least twice a month. I paid for the gas, and he furnished the car. Following high school graduation, Ken attended Westminster College and Oklahoma Law School. We had planned to room together at OU Law School, but when I did not get a scholarship to OU and did get a scholarship to KU, I elected to stay at KU for law school. Ken has practiced law for many years, and now pursues lobbying activities for a variety of oil and gas companies. He lives in the Houston area with his wife, Anna Lee. They have three children and many grandchildren.

Other close friends in high school included John Jones and his twin sister, Jan. John and Jan came to Edison just before our sophomore year in high school. John was elected president of the Edison Student Council as a senior and served that year as the vice president of Key Club International, requiring him to travel more than 50,000 miles his senior year. After college John graduated from law school and the international school of finance in Phoenix. He pursued a career in international banking that has taken him all over the world. His sister, Jan, married David Curnutt, our sophomore class president. They later divorced.

High school was a time of many honors for me. I was elected December Boy of the Month my senior year and was voted Hardest Worker in our high school class of 765 students. The high school newspaper staff voted me Most Outstanding Senior.

My angels were all around, especially in the disappointments. Losing the elections as Key Club President and Senior Class President were lows. Not succeeding in basketball was hard, but not achieving success in baseball was the worst. Each disappointment was followed by success in another area. By overcoming high school disappointments, I grew stronger. I learned to work hard and strive for perfection. I learned that it was the process of striving to achieve high goals, not the achievement of those goals, that defined success. High school was a terrific base upon which my life at Kansas University would rest.

Kansas University
1961-1965

I had hoped to attend Washington & Lee University in Lexington, VA. Washington & Lee was the school selected by Gene Brown, the senior with whom I traveled to Toronto to the Key Club International convention. Washington & Lee is the picture of what I thought college should be. It was a small, private men-only school located on a beautiful campus in a small southern Virginia town surrounded by great tradition and an excellent academic reputation. While I was accepted, I simply could not afford W & L without a scholarship, which I did not receive.

In March 1961, I began to consider alternative colleges. I did not want to go to either to OSU or OU, since all my friends were going to one of those two schools and since both schools enjoyed a world-class party school reputation. I had worked too hard and saved too long to squander my education at a party school.

One weekend my parents and I drove to Lawrence, KS, to visit the University of Kansas. It is a beautiful university on top of the only hill in Kansas. The weather was beautiful. Spring had sprung. The fragrance of lilacs filled the air, and the campus was exciting and alive. I went into Strong Hall to obtain a map of the campus, and the admissions director was in his office. We talked for fifteen minutes, and he introduced me to Dean Woodruff, the dean of men. I was welcomed into the KU family that Saturday morning. When I got home from school on Monday, I had a personal letter from each of these two men, inviting me to become a member of the KU stu-

23

dent body. I decided that if they were that nice to someone who had not even applied, whose record they had not seen, that was where I wanted to go to school.

In late June following high school graduation, Dad invited me to have lunch with him at Nelson's Buffeteria, a Tulsa landmark. We always had chicken fried steak, green beans, mashed potatoes and gravy and lemon pie. Having lunch with Dad was an annual event, but it was very special for me and for Dad. It gave Dad an opportunity to show off his sons. After lunch, as we were walking back to his office, we met Ed Strong. Ed had been a Scout master at Troop 37 after I finished my Scouting experience. Ed was a Colonel in the Army Reserves. He urged me to sign up for Army ROTC. While most land grant colleges, including OU and OSU, required men to take two years of ROTC, ROTC was voluntary at KU. Nevertheless, because Ed Strong said it would be an easy A, I decided to sign up. This seemingly insignificant decision for all the wrong reasons became a defining moment for me, because the decision to sign up for ROTC ultimately kept me out of Vietnam and possibly even saved my life.

As a freshman at KU, I lived in J. R. Pearson dormitory. My roommate was a senior sanitary engineering student named Laverne. He was wing counselor for our floor, and he was a heavy smoker. He had no personality, and we had nothing in common. Several freshman football and basketball players lived on my wing. I studied hard, made good grades, quizzed out of Calculus I and enjoyed the year very much.

Our dorm wing had an intramural B basketball team, which consisted of mostly red-shirt freshman football players and me. I was the only one on the team who was not a scholarship athlete. We were pretty damn good, extremely powerful and incredibly rough. Larry Ledford, a Kansas high school All State halfback, weighing 220 and built like a fireplug, was hell on the backboards. Our team could not shoot very well, but we won the B non-fraternity tournament.

Larry was joyous, an excellent football player and fun to be around. On the day he got red-shirted on the football team, Larry came in totally drunk at about 2:00 a.m. When he tried to get a drink of water from the water fountain across the hall from my dorm room, nothing happened, so he simply lifted the fountain out of the wall. Water gushed everywhere. More than four inches of water covered my floor, and water seeped down through the light fixtures onto the cafeteria below. I helped Larry get in bed and tried to get the water stopped. I still do not know if anyone ever found out who caused the water fountain to be disconnected from the wall.

I remember one Saturday, walking to a Medieval History class at 7:30 a.m., when the temperature was below zero and there was a strong wind blowing out of the north. Only a handful of the 58 students showed up that day. I was there, and that is probably why I got an A in the class. I also remember my shock when I got a D+ on my first mid-term English paper. As it turned out, there were only three passing grades, all D's, out of the 38 students in my freshman English class. Despite the initial D+, I ultimately got a B in the class. There were no A's.

My sophomore year at KU was quite different. I pledged Beta Theta Pi fraternity and moved into the house. The "Butt Hut" is a special place. The brothers said, "We were all studs in high school," and indeed most of us were. There were twenty three in my pledge class, and virtually every one of them did graduate work in pharmacy, law, medicine, nuclear physics, organic chemistry or some other major academic discipline. Our Beta chapter had the best cumulative grade point average for any fraternity chapter in the nation for two of the three years I was in the House. We had been one of the top ten chapters academically for several years. We also won the fraternity, as well as Hill championships in A football, B football, A basketball, B basketball and several other sports.

I got to catch on our A softball team, which won the fraternity championship all three years I was in the house but which also lost the Hill championship to the law school team all three years. Our A and B teams in football and basketball practiced as much as any high school team practiced. My senior year, we decided to have a B-2 football team, whose objective was to never practice except during games. Our quarterback was John Grantham, a high school All-State quarterback and a Big Eight singles tennis champion. We won every game except for the fraternity B football championship, which we lost to the other Beta B team, 20 to 14. We had a great time in intramurals.

I have many fond memories of the Beta House. As pledges, every two or three days, we were commanded to "hit a brace" on the second floor landing or in the dining room. Discipline for unclean rooms or just generally for harassment was meted out randomly during these sessions. If a pledge brother screwed up, the whole pledge class paid the price. We did more push-ups, more sit-ups and more just plain exercise than I thought was even possible. I think one of the reasons our fraternity did so well in intramurals was that the freshmen were in terrific shape.

As pledges, we also were required to move rooms on random occasions, usually every two or three weeks but sometimes twice in one evening. The purpose of these moves was so that the pledges could meet and live with all of the actives in the house. These moves were chaotic. At approximately 10:15 p.m., the actives would yell out "hit a brace" on the second floor landing. The pledge trainer would simply walk between the pledges and re-assign rooms. He would give us ten minutes to move. Failure to have all of our things moved in time resulted in having to do push-ups and more push-ups. After the first two or three moves, we became very proficient at moving. We kept all of our books and belongings in our drawers in boxes, so that we could pick up the boxes and moved them very quickly. It is amazing that twenty-three guys can move rooms in ten minutes and be studying ten minutes later.

Academics were stressed beyond everything to the Betas. If anyone was struggling, someone helped his brother out. Our pledge class had a 3.52 cumulative grade point average the first semester we pledged, while our whole House had a 3.28 cumulative grade average for the year in which we pledged.

We participated in Rock Chalk Reviews, nightly singing around the piano in the trophy room, intramural sports and "kill sessions" before each game for the A and B games, especially during championship week. All are vivid memories which I cherish today. The Betas always went together to "Ra-Ra Hill functions" (such as varsity football and basketball games). We did not take dates or non-Beta friends. We sat with other Betas. We stayed together. As such, we were viewed as pretty weird by others on campus.

Rock Chalk Review was a wonderful, joyously entertaining experience. The participants included one fraternity and one sorority whose members worked together to write the satirical script, sing the sarcastic songs and dance the dances, all of which had to be original. During my three years in the House, we won Rock Chalk Review each year. My brothers were not only terrific athletes, but they were also incredibly talented musically and theatrically.

Our pledge class, like all fraternity pledge classes, got to "walk out" of the house one weekend in February just before initiation. Most fraternity pledge classes go to another campus and stay at their chapter's fraternity house over the weekend. The pledge "sneak" usually lasted one weekend, with the pledges returning to their own campus and own fraternity house late Sunday evening.

Our pledge class walked out of the House, not for a weekend but for fifteen days. We rented a vacant house near the KU campus and twenty-three mattresses. Mrs. Meyers, our house mother, and Jake Hayes, our handyman, brought our mail and meals to us each day. To the entire university, we were still living in the House. We participated in intramural sports during this time, including fraternity and Hill championships in basketball, just like we lived in the

House. Not one single member of my pledge class missed a single class. Thank God no one got hurt!

Unlike all other fraternity houses, girls not engaged or pinned to a Beta were not permitted in the Beta House. The Turkey Pull was the one exception. The Turkey Pull was an annual Christmas party dating back to the 1880s. The House was literally transformed into a medieval forest. It was unbelievable how much greenery was used, how much work the decorations took and how excited the girls were to get a chance to come into the hallowed halls of the Beta House. I attended five Turkey Pulls, three as a member of the House and two as a waiter who waited tables during this event.

KU Betas were the oldest fraternity chapter west of the Mississippi. The Beta House was the Kansas territorial governor's mansion in 1860s. Legend has it that around Christmas in the 1880s, some brothers went out and "pulled" (stole) two turkeys for Christmas dinner. A tradition was begun. Since that first "turkey pull," pledges repeated this theft annually. Fortunately, no one to my knowledge has ever been caught for "pulling any turkeys," but several times local turkey farmers have fired shots into the air to scare off the intruders. Almost everyone got covered with turkey shit my senior year when the pledges returned with two huge turkeys which they let loose in the "roost," the top floor of the Beta House where everybody in the House slept. After that experience, I know exactly why birds are called "fowl."

Serenades of sorority houses occurred when a brother in our House became engaged or pinned to a member of the sorority. Our entire House would serenade the girl at her house. Other fraternities took this occasion to dress up in tuxedos. The Betas looked like a motley crew, but the Betas always sounded great, despite their appearance.

Because the Betas always won the scholarship trophy and usually won fraternity intramurals and Rock Chalk Review, everyone who was not a Beta wanted to beat us. One Saturday morning after a wonderfully beautiful six-inch snow, the time came for action by the non-Betas. After lunch, when most of the Betas were in the library on the Hill "booking it," a rumble began to sound in the distance. The rumble turned out to be more than 500 fraternity and sorority members coming from the west campus east down 14th Street to engage the Betas in one massive snowball fight. There were only thirteen of us in the House at the time to defend the Betas honor. We were outgunned, out numbered and out maneuvered. Someone with a megaphone counted out "one, two, three," and everybody in the crowd threw snowballs simultaneously. At the end of the day, there were several broken windows, a number of black eyes, one busted collarbone and a couple broken arms. Beta pride was a little crushed. Except for an area about 500 feet around the Beta House, everything remained beautifully white in Lawrence, but within that circle, the ground was black. TV cameras filmed the event for the late night news that night, announcing the defeat under the caption, "Betas Finally Lose." Despite the fact that we were soundly defeated, it was a lot of fun and a terrific memory.

I attended every home freshman and varsity basketball game during my seven years at KU. I remember watching TV when KU and Texas Southern played for the chance to be in the "Final Four." The triple overtime shot by Jo Jo White just across at half court line went in at the buzzer, only to have Jo Jo's foot touching the out of bounds line, denying KU a Final Four appearance. That Texas Southern team was composed of mostly black players. They started all black players against Coach Adolph Rupp's Wildcats from Kentucky, something that had never been done before. Texas Southern won the national championship. That Final Four victory did much to ensure that black athletes would never again be denied varsity participation because of the color of their skin.

I also attended most of the home football games. I saw John Haddell, Curtis McClinton, Bobby Douglas, John Riggins and the great Gale Sayers, who was in my ROTC class as a freshman.

During one KU football game against OU my senior year (1964), Gale Sayers ran the opening kickoff back ninety seven yards for a touchdown. For the next fifty eight minutes, OU beat KU like a drum all over the field. However, OU only scored fourteen points. With less than a minute to play, Bobby Scahan, Gayle Sayers and Junior Riggins moved the ball to the OU forty yard line. With only seconds on the clock, Bobby threw a Hail Mary pass into the north end zone. I do not recall which Jayhawk caught the ball, but the score was 14 to 13. KU elected to attempt a two point conversion, instead of kicking an extra point to tie the game. Miraculously, KU scored two points, and the Jayhawks won 15 to 14. Unbelievable!

I was elected to Sachem Circle, the local Omicron Delta Kappa national men's senior leadership society. I was also elected vice president of the Beta House and later pledge trainer second semester of my senior year. One night just before the pledges were initiated, I woke in the Roost with a live grass snake in my bed. Jake, our sixty-five year-old "house boy" and a close friend of every Beta who live in the House, just about jumped out of his skin when he saw the snake. So did I. The pledges had hell to pay that night, even though they never admitted the prank. It ended up being one of the funniest stories I recall during pledging, even though the joke was on me. Beta House justice was invoked, the pledges were responsible. There was no trial, no witnesses, no explanation, no justification, no defense, no confrontation, no cross-examination, no hearing, just judgment, a guilty verdict. That notion of justice never seemed quite right to me, but whoever promised "fair" in fraternity justice? Justice was swift and sure. Angels kept the snake away from me physically, but I still remember that damn snake in my bed. Actually, it was pretty funny after I got over freaking out.

KU ROTC
1961-1965

E ven though KU is a land grant university, ROTC was not mandatory. Choosing to sign up for ROTC proved to be an amazing
blessing. My father worked in the oil patch during World War II, a
critical industry, so he was not allowed to join the military. His skills
were too important out in the oil patch for him to be in uniform. My
older brother missed military service, because in 1963 he was married and married men were not drafted. By 1965, Phil had a son and
men with children were then not drafted. So I was the first in my
family to be in the military. By 1968, the United States had more
than 650,000 troops in Vietnam, and military service was required
of all able men in accordance with the draft then in effect. Every
male scrambled to avoid the draft or to schedule military service in
a prudent way. Because I joined ROTC in 1961, I did not go through
the uncertainty that others experienced with a low draft number. I
was already in the Army.

   I decided to stay in ROTC my junior year for two reasons: I
received an award at the end of my sophomore year, and I began to
receive $43 a month beginning in the fall of my junior year at KU.
While the money does not seem like much today, it meant a lot to me
then, because it helped finance my last two years as an undergraduate
at KU. My decision to continue in ROTC proved to be a defining
moment for me. ROTC was no longer a one-hour A, but now it was
a three-hour course that required significant effort. Upper classmen

were required to take responsibility for drill sessions and for other military related projects.

Before going to ROTC summer camp in 1964, the regular Army officers who were teaching ROTC at KU arranged a field exercise one weekend in mid-April. The story was that enemy airborne troops were going to be dropped into an area to take control of a certain bridge south of Lawrence, KS. Our job, as ROTC military students, was to defend and hold the bridge. Of course, we had no idea what we were doing but we played along. This was an all night exercise. The ROTC students took turns guarding the bridge. I was company commander in charge of one bridge detail.

Paratroopers did in fact parachute into the open field near the bridge. Our troops guarded both sides of the bridge. However, while I was inspecting the "soldiers" on one side of the bridge at about 2:00 a.m., I heard the sound of a train coming from the distance. The train was coming very fast. No one told us that the railroad bridge was active. I was caught in the middle of the bridge with no where to go, and the train speeding toward me.

The bridge was about 100 feet above the water and about 300 feet long. There was simply no time for me to get to either end of the bridge before the train came. I climbed over the fence and stood on a small concrete pillar that held the bridge up with my face inches away from the train as it sped by. No one was hurt. No incident report was ever made. Officially my near death experience did not even happen. Shortly after the train sped by, an attack by the insurgents took over the bridge, overpowering our meager defense. I was glad to be alive, so I did not get too excited about the mock "attack."

I attended ROTC training camp at Fort Riley, KS, for eight weeks during the summer of 1964. The weather was unbearably hot that summer. It was so hot that when mealtime came, I drank cold milk as fast as I could. After the milk, I could not bear to eat anything else. I lost about twenty five pounds in eight weeks, even though the food was excellent; and there was lots of it. It was so hot that for a couple weeks we were awakened at 2:00 a.m., did our physical exercises in the dark and finished our training sessions by 11:00 a.m. This schedule enabled Ray Siegfried, a friend of mine from Tulsa, to teach me how to drink beer.

The ROTC summer camp experiences were interesting and in some ways life changing. The leadership responsibilities were passed around to each of the student/cadets. When it was my responsibility to be the leader, I studied the materials and knew what was to be taught. However, when it was not my turn to be a leader, I like all the other guys, did not even read the lesson plan. I goofed off. This pattern of irresponsibility proved very embarrassing.

Our company was assigned to go on a four and a half mile forced march with full packs on our backs during the hottest part of the day. It was not my day to lead, since I had been the company commander the day before. However, fifty yards into the forced march, there was a simulated explosion behind me. The regular Army officer in charge tapped me on the shoulder and said, "Slicker, your commander has just been killed by a mine. You're in charge." I was stunned and totally unprepared. It was my day to skate, not to lead. I had not read the materials. I simply was unprepared.

I got our entire battalion of more than 350 guys lost in sweltering 100 plus degree heat. Our battalion was followed by ambulances and doctors to ensure that no one suffered heatstroke or other heat related injuries. Embarrassingly, we arrived at our destination more than three hours late. My angels kept me and the other 350 men safe. Thank God no one got hurt! What a lesson! Never again did I not read the lesson materials.

"Dream day" at Fort Riley was a defining moment for me also. Each ROTC cadet was allowed to explore the various opportunities the Army offered. I went to the Judge Advocate General Corps tent, because by this time I had decided to attend law school after graduation. CPT Kent McCoin, my Dallas Key Club friend, was there to explain various JAGC programs, including the Excess Leave

33

Program. If accepted, the ROTC cadet would be assured of receiving a JAGC commission if he graduated from law school and if he passed the bar. To get in the Program, the ROTC cadet was required to: (1) be selected to be a distinguished military graduate (top ten percent of his ROTC class); (2) agree to accept a Regular Army commission upon graduation (a commission that had no ending date of service and required a resignation to leave the service as opposed to a reserve commission that had an ending date of service); and (3) agree to serve an additional six months of active duty for each year of Excess Leave. Prior to ROTC summer camp, I had never heard of the Excess Leave Program, but it was perfect for me. I was accepted into the Excess Leave Program upon my return to KU in the Fall of 1964. Once again, this decision proved to be a defining moment for me, since it set the tone for my entire military experience.

ROTC summer camp ended with a series of leadership tests in the field. Each cadet was given three separate problems and was graded on his reaction. I received high marks, because I made decisive decisions, but almost all of my decisions were wrong. One leadership test involved a night guard duty assignment. At 2:00 a.m., I was standing guard and a voice called out, "Help me, help me." I stayed on my guard post without going to this soldier's aid. I did the right thing according to the Army book, because I was protecting a larger group on guard duty. But every emotion I had said I should have gone to help the wounded comrade.

Another test resulted in me losing my entire squad. Prior to this exercise, we were issued bayonets for the daytime exercise. I anticipated some kind of hand-to-hand combat activity instead of a minefield, though one of our classes did involve minefield training. I led a squad of five men into a suspected enemy position. Suddenly, I heard an explosion behind me, and I ordered the squad to charge, which they did. We were supposed to drop down and probe for mines. Charging in a mine field, which is usually covered by a machine gun, might get someone a metal for bravery but would almost surely result in the death of many squad members. I acted quickly and decisively, so I got a good grade, but I my actions were exactly the wrong thing to do. I knew right then that I was not cut out to lead men in combat. I was meant to be a JAGC officer, a staff officer working in the office away from the enemy, using legal and procedural means to win battles of the mind, rather than guns on the battle field. Angels again kept me out of the field and out of the line of fire. Thank you, God.

KU Law School
1965-1968

I took a Business Law class in the KU Business School my last semester as an undergraduate at KU. It was the only class I really studied. I knew the material cold, but I got a D+ on the mid-term exam. I had not gotten less than a B in any class at KU, except for eleven hours of C in French. I had no idea why I did not receive an A on the Business Law mid-term, since I thought I maxed the exam. If I could not do better than a D+ on a mid-term exam in Business Law, how would I even pass a law school class?

The third-year law student who graded the Business Law exam papers spent over an hour with me, explaining why I did not receive a better grade. It was the best hour I ever spent. He told me how a lawyer would have answered the questions and how I would be expected to write like a lawyer in law school. This experience was a defining moment for me, since I started law school knowing how to write an exam paper. Angels guided me into that Business Law class and sat with me as I learned how to write. I got an A+ on each of the remaining Business Law exams, and I got an A in the Business Law class. I would be a law student for the next three years.

Upon graduation from KU, I accepted a Regular Army commission and accepted admission into the JAGC Excess Leave Program. My basic branch was artillery, and I was assigned to Fort Sill, OK. I got paid when I worked at Fort Sill, but otherwise I was on an unpaid non-active status. I was assigned to the Military Justice Division in the office of the Staff Judge Advocate. I watched numerous general and special court-martial cases. I helped the lawyers prepare for trial in some cases. I reviewed the transcript of many trials. I even defended several alleged "preps" in special court-martial cases while I was a law student. Fort Sill was a great experience for me.

I intended to enter law school at the University of Oklahoma, but God and my lack of money changed all that. Ken Burton, my best friend in high school, and I planned to room together at OU. However, OU had a policy that no scholarships would be granted to first year law students. Scholarships were reserved for law students that demonstrated promise during their first year of law school. KU awarded scholarships to first year law students, but not to third year law students. I got a scholarship to KU, so I stayed there for law school. That was a great decision. My angels were working overtime for me in selecting the best law school for me to attend.

I supplemented that scholarship by waiting tables at the Theta House, the sorority house next to the Beta House, just three blocks from the law school. I also taught three semesters of eight one-hour classes in Western Civilization, a class which surveyed the ideas of the great writers of western thought. Every student at KU, regardless of department, was required to take and pass Western Civilization.

My first law school class at KU was in Property Law taught by Dean James Logan, later a federal judge on the 10th Circuit Court of Appeals in Denver. He opened the class by saying, "Look around. A third of you will not be here next semester." All of us were scared to death, including me. Not quite that many dropped out, but many did.

I loved law school. Finally, I was doing something real, reading about real cases, real people and real problems. I was eager, hard working, diligent and committed, and I knew how to write because of my Business Law class experience the semester before. My first final exam was in Contracts. The first day of my second semester Contracts class, Professor Schurtz read my answer to the first question as an example of A work. Unfortunately, my answer to question one left me insufficient time to write the same quality answers to questions two through four.

Consequently, I got a B, not an A, in Contracts I. I never made that mistake again, but I was launched on my path to a career in the law.

At the end of my first year in law school, I was selected to be on the KU Law Review staff, one of twelve in my class of 135 to receive such an honor. Law Review was a 40 to 50 hour a week non-paying job, but that is where I really learned to write like a lawyer. Each law review member had to write at least two case notes during his second year and one case note plus one major comment during his third year. Each law review student reviewed, criticized, checked citations for, re-wrote, edited and marked up articles submitted by professors and distinguished lawyers for publication. Many of the articles written were written by my own KU professors. None of my teachers liked my comments, but the negotiations that led to a compromise in the language and content of the proposed papers helped me tremendously in dealing with other difficult issues later. Law Review allowed me to learn by doing. My senior comment was voted the best student paper written that year. I served as Note Editor my second year and as Comment Editor and Associate Editor-in-Chief my third year. That experience was invaluable and extremely helpful to me in seeking employment later. Angels were everywhere around me during my law school experiences.

I remember smoking a pipe my first year of law school, because I thought it was cool. I liked the smell of the tobacco, but I hated the taste and the smoke. I also hated burning small holes in all my shirts because of smoldering ashes flying from my pipe. There was so much to manage and so little enjoyment. I finally gave up smoking a pipe after two or three months. I never smoked cigarettes or cigars, largely because my father's three-pack-a-day habit resulted in his heart attack and early death. I stopped smoking my pipe the same day I decided to stop drinking coffee. A group of us would gather at the KU Student Union following class to discuss what took place in class or what was to take place in the next class. I enjoyed the camaraderie, but I did not like the taste of the coffee. I liked its smell, but I preferred something cold, not hot. To this day, I drink fewer than four or five cups of coffee a year.

One funny event occurred during my last class during my second year of law school. Dean Logan taught Trusts and Estates. He was an expert in the area. We were using his case book. He was the youngest law school dean in the United States at the time; and he was a strong advocate of student attendance in law school classes. He hated law students missing class, since he thought missing a class was an insult to the professor and a failure on the student's part to take advantage of the intellectual combat that took place during class.

Bill Mills was a self-proclaimed party animal as a KU undergraduate. By his own admission, he hardly ever attended an undergraduate class. Three days before his last law school class, he boasted in the Student Union to some of his classmates that he had never missed a law school class. No one could believe it, since everyone missed at least one class. His classmates decided to cure that problem. The plan was to handcuff him to the bronze statue of Jimmy Green in front of the law school building just before his last law school class, so that he would miss at least one class in law school.

The law school was housed in an old colonial style building with concrete columns and twelve steps leading up to its entrance. The school was situated between the freshman girls' dormitories and the Student Union on the north and the rest of the campus on the south and west. For freshman girls to get to class, they had to pass in front of the law school. It was a tradition for the law students to sit on the law school steps before and after class to watch the girls go by. Dean Logan heard about the prank and decided to play along. Dean Logan taught the Trusts and Estates Class on the steps in front of the law school with Mr. Mills handcuffed behind him. Photographers drove by and took pictures that were later printed in the national wire services and even were printed in the *London Times*. The Dean Logan's attendance policy was enforced, Mr. Mills graduated without ever missing a law school class, and we had a great laugh.

I won many honors at KU law school. I was elected outstanding graduate out of one hundred and sixteen Phi Delta Phi members in my class. I was elected to the Order of the Coif, which honors the top ten percent of law students in each class. I graduated with highest distinction, third in my class out 135 students. I won books for the best exam paper in five of my classes. I got to work with Professor Paul Wilson, the Assistant Attorney General of Kansas who argued *Brown v. Board of Education of Topeka* before the United States Supreme Court. I was his Associate Editor of the Criminal Law Journal, a publication of the American Bar Association. I made many friends and learned each day to love the law and to study hard. My angels helped me achieve goals beyond my wildest dreams in law school.

In December 1967, I asked one of my Western Civilization students fix me up with one of her sorority sisters. Claudia Fincham was a member of Delta Delta Delta, a beautiful violin major. I was smitten immediately. Our first date consisted of a pre-party before a KU basketball game. On the second date, I was privileged to watch Claudia play her senior violin recital. I was overwhelmed. The third date scheduled for 8:30 p.m. on Thursday was a disaster. She simply did not show up. She called me about 12:30 a.m. to say she went to drink beer with some other friends. Six months later we were married.

The week of our marriage consisted of me taking the Kansas bar examination in Topeka on Monday and Tuesday, being sworn in to practice law before the Kansas Supreme Court as a member of the Kansas Bar on Wednesday, attending the rehearsal dinner for our wedding in Pratt on Friday, getting married in Pratt on Saturday and driving to our honeymoon destination Saturday night.

We spent the first week of our marriage at TanTerra Resort on the Lake of the Ozarks before I reported for active duty at Fort Sill in

Lawton, Oklahoma. Claudia changed from being a violin major her senior year to majoring in music education, so she did not finish her degree. While Claudia has earned more college credits than I have, she did not do her student teaching. Instead, she chose to come with me to Fort Sill and then to Charlottesville, VA, for JAGC School, rather than staying in Kansas to complete her student teaching.

The Army
1965-1972

Claudia and I settled into a neat one bedroom apartment in Lawton. We would be in Lawton until I received orders to attend the Army's JAGC basic school held at the University of Virginia Law School from September to December 1968.

My first general court-martial case involved a young soldier charged with AWOL for more than sixty days and disobedience of a superior officer. My client was a seventeen year old kid from Arkansas, who was given the choice between entering the Army or serving time in prison. He chose the Army. He had gone home on leave after basic artillery training, gotten into a bar room brawl and been incarcerated in a local jail as a material witness in a murder case for most of his AWOL time. I believe he was probably the perpetrator of the knife fight, but no one said so. He was returned to Fort Sill on a Thursday, the day before the post commander made his weekly inspection of the Fort Sill stockade.

During that inspection, my client was ordered to step forward. However, my client and eight other more hardened offenders refused to step forward. I am convinced that my client simply wanted to get attention, since it was his first day in lock up, and he felt he needed some stature with the other prisoners. The general was not amused, but my client was never charged with disrespect for this offense. On three successive nights about two weeks before trial, my client used a razor blade on his arms. I do not believe that he was trying to kill himself, and neither did the Army shrink, who concluded that my client's numerous cuts on his arms were additional attempts simply to get attention. He got my attention, but it did not do him much good.

I explained to him in great detail his options: to plead guilty or to plead not guilty and to assert defenses to the AWOL charge, because of his incarceration and to advance other theories of defense. After repeated conversations, my client elected to plead guilty and to seek a minimal sentence from the court-martial. I had been advised that he was being held as a material witness in Arkansas in a bar room knife fight and murder, but no one else in the bar room brawl would talk.

I negotiated a very favorable plea bargain. Military trials are bifurcated into two separate phases: (1) guilt or innocence; and (2) sentencing. In plea bargains, the accused gets the benefit of the deal made or the sentence given by the court, whichever is less.

We went to trial wearing Army green uniforms in the middle of September, when the official uniform was short sleeve khakis. I got the judge's permission to wear greens to avoid the Court seeing all the bandages on my client's arms. This proved to be a good decision. My client plead guilty, got a sentence of ten months in jail and no discharge. This sentence was better than the one year plus a bad conduct discharge deal in his negotiated plea, so he got the benefit of what the court's sentence was.

On appeal, my client told the appellate defense counsel that I had not advised him of his right to plead not guilty or any of his other rights. No one called me to confirm or deny his lies, so my client got a reduced sentence because of his lies. Welcome to the real world where clients lie, and lawyers get blamed!

In early September 1968, Claudia and I journeyed to Charlottesville, VA, to attend the twelve-week JAGC Basic Course. When a new officer enters the Army, he is required to attend the basic course in his branch. The purpose of this course is to provide information and instruction to the new officer regarding his duties and responsibilities and the substantive nature of his future work. I had been in contact with Sid Dunagan, whom I knew through Boy Scouts in Tulsa. I arranged for Sid and his wife, Lynn, to stay in the same apartment complex in Charlottesville where Claudia and I were to stay. Lynn gave birth to her first son while we were there with them. Sid is a lawyer with Gable & Gotwals in Oklahoma City now and recently served a year as President of the Oklahoma Bar Association. Lynn is deceased.

The JAGC basic class taught military law with an emphasis upon criminal law, the rules of evidence, military procedure and discipline, and some instruction on military procurement and administrative law. My basic class consisted of 102 new captains, 77 of whom graduated first in their law school class. This was 1968, shortly after the devastating TET offensive in Vietnam earlier in the spring. The United States had more than 650,000 troops in Vietnam. Everyone scrambled to make inevitable military service the best experience possible.

CPT John Freidenberger was in charge of JAGC captains' initial assignments. Fortunately for me, John was my brother Phil's best friend in high school. Also fortunately for me, during the summer of 1968, John attended the ROTC dream day at Fort Sill, Oklahoma. I was assigned to escort John to and from the ROTC encampment. This gave me an opportunity to renew our friendship and to discuss my hopes and desires for my time in the military. There were two choice assignments, one at Fort Ord, CA, and the other at Fort Lewis, WA. Almost every person in my JAGC class requested a West Coast assignment, but only three of us got one of those choice assignments. I was assigned to Fort Lewis.

The most memorable event which occurred while we attended JAGC school class was our trip to Washington, DC, where all of the new captains were sworn in to practice before the United States Court of Military Appeals. During that trip, we toured the United States Capitol, the United States Supreme Court, Arlington National Cemetery and the Smithsonian Air and Space Museum. Following graduation, we were granted two weeks leave, so that we could spend the Christmas holidays with our families.

Fort Lewis
1969

My first day at Fort Lewis was memorable. It was a beautiful January day. The sun was radiant. The temperature was 65 degrees, though it had snowed briefly the evening before. After signing in for duty, I reported to COL Dennis York, the Staff Judge Advocate. COL York was a career military officer, a full colonel and a fine lawyer. He had just returned from three years in Europe. Fort Lewis would be his last assignment before his retirement. Within a few minutes of my welcome, COL York said that I should expect to be at Fort Lewis no longer than a year. COL York said that I would be assigned to Vietnam, unless I took positive steps to go elsewhere. If I desired to go to Germany, I should say so right then, and he would make it happen. I told him I wanted to go Germany. Within fifteen minutes after reporting for my first duty assignment, I was already making plans for my next assignment. This was incredibly unusual and more evidence that angels surrounded me. Less than nine months earlier, when I proposed to marry Claudia, I told her then that I expected to be in the United States for a year and that I anticipated an assignment to Germany for three years after that. How prophetic!

There were seventeen captains in the JAGC office at Fort Lewis. Most were assigned to prosecute and defend criminal cases. I was initially assigned to help soldiers with personal affairs not involving court-martial charges. My first day at work I met Robert Cheatum, a West Virginia law school graduate, and Charlie Senn, a former football standout at Ohio State University and a terrific lawyer. I said we should form a law firm, "Slicker, Cheatum & Senn." Everyone laughed.

Fort Lewis is a large Army installation whose primary function then was to provide Advanced Infantry Training to young Army recruits assigned to Vietnam. AIT consisted of sixteen weeks of training to supplement the eight week basic training all soldiers received. For many, Fort Lewis was the last place in the United States they would see, because immediately after completing AIT, they were flown to Vietnam. Many came back in a body bag.

I defended or prosecuted more than 100 special and general court-martial cases while at Fort Lewis. For some reason, a rash of conscientious objector cases occurred during my time there. These cases were brought against soldiers who refused to board the airplane for Vietnam, resulting in an order from a non-commissioned officer followed by an order from a commissioned officer to get on the plane. The trials were relatively simple. These cases were easy to prosecute, and there were few if any defenses to the disobedience charges.

My trial judge, COL Lee, a thirty-year Army veteran, was your basic redneck from Mississippi. He called these conscientious objector cases "conscientious coward" cases. The soldiers accused of disobedience in these cases were typically college graduates, who had extensive and deep religious beliefs and experiences and who simply did not believe it was proper for the US to be fighting in Vietnam. Unfortunately, strongly held beliefs that a particular war is wrong do not qualify for conscientious objector status and is not a defense to disobedience of a lawful order. The order is presumptively lawful and the failure to obey the order is presumptively unlawful.

I remember three specific conscientious objector cases. One involved a solider from California who told me that he was a Marlanian, a person who follows the spiritual leader, Marla, this soldier's mother. Marla led a small group of religious zealots whose principal religious beliefs were that there were four great people, divinely appointed by God in the history of man. The first was Moses. The second was Jesus. The third was Einstein, and the fourth was Marla. I requested that Marla be produced as a defense witness. Following his conviction, I call both the accused and his mother as mitigation witnesses. Marla was a huge, red-headed woman who wore long braided pigtails. If she carried a spear in her hand, she would have been perfect for a Wagnerian opera. She testified about her religious revelations, the scope and extent of the beliefs of her "church" and the extent of her son's involvement in her church activities. She sought compassion from the court. It was difficult for the jury to remain composed without laughing. Her testimony was effective, and her son received the lightest sentence of any soldier I defended in these conscientious objector cases.

The second case involved an Orthodox Jewish soldier from New York City. Given the history of the Jewish people, it is difficult to imagine contending that this soldier's religious beliefs allowed him to claim to be opposed to all wars. Nevertheless, that was his contention, which if true, entitled him to conscientious objector status. Several of the elders from his Orthodox Jewish synagogue appeared as defense witnesses to support his effort. Fortunately for him, COL Lee was on annual leave. COL Snyder, a trial judge from California, was assigned to hear the case.

As I had routinely done in the past, I made a motion to dismiss the charges, arguing that the government had failed to follow Department of Army Regulations in processing of the defendant's request for conscientious objector status. I supported that argument with recent Supreme Court cases in which the Court had defined what a conscientious objector was. None of the commanders who decided against the application of this soldier had ever heard of the cases, the Army regulations did not include the substantive law applicable to such decisions, and the applications were routinely denied without a finding of facts that contravened the criteria for consciousness objector status. COL Lee was never amused by this argument. He never granted my motion to dismiss based upon this argument. COL Snyder, on the other hand, had never heard this argument, and he was intrigued. At the end of evidence on my motion in which I called three of the commanders at Fort Lewis who had recommended denial of the application for the Jewish soldier accused in this case, COL Snyder granted the motion to dismiss and ordered this solider be released from the Army on the grounds that he qualified for conscientious objector status.

Upon COL Lee's return from vacation, he was furious. It is ironic that of the twelve or fifteen other soldiers who expressed deep religious opposition to all wars, my motion was granted in only one case, a case involving a Jewish solider from NYC whose religious history and experience defied the rational conclusion that he was opposed to ALL wars. Go figure!

I experienced one other victory in the conscientious objector cases. This case involved 1LT David Bean. David was an honors graduate of West Point who had served his first one-year tour of duty in Germany as a general's aide. He was ordered to Vietnam. David was from Beaumont, TX, the son of the business manager of the local newspaper. In the South, military service is close to godliness. Being accepted to West Point and graduating with honors is an experience revered by most Southerners. To assert that a West Point graduate, who had received a free education at one of America's finest military schools, was a conscientious objector defied logic and devalued the West Point experience.

When David returned home from Germany, he told his parents and his fiancé that he simply could not in good conscience lead men in battle and fight a war in Vietnam. He reported to Fort Sam Houston in San Antonio, the closest major military installation to Beaumont, expressing his deeply felt beliefs. After a week of being hot boxed by other West Point graduates, including the four star Commanding General of the Fifth US Army, David was placed on the general's plane between two armed first sergeants (a gross violation of military protocol) and flown to Fort Lewis, WA, where he would be ordered to go to Vietnam the next day. My general was alerted. My Staff Judge Advocate called me to visit with David upon his arrival.

Under US Army regulations, a request for conscientious objector status triggers a personnel action which must be resolved before any change in assignment could take place. David arrived in my Fort Lewis office at about 4 p.m. on a Thursday. From 4:00 p.m. to 7:00 p.m. that day, I got to know him and learned about his background and beliefs. Throughout his four years at West Point, he had traveled almost 100 miles every Sunday to teach Sunday school to high school students at a Presbyterian church in downtown New York City. After listening to him express his views, I told him that I believed that he qualified for conscientious objector status.

David never considered himself to be a conscientious objector and never even thought about filing a request for relief from the service on the basis of his conscientious objection to all war. I gave David copies of the three most recent United States Supreme Court cases defining what it means to be a "conscientious objector," which specifically stated the rules and criteria required to be used in determining whether a person is entitled to dismissal from the service as a conscientious objector. I requested that David read these cases and report to me at 7:00 a.m. the next morning. He was scheduled for departure to Vietnam later that day.

David came to my office at 7 a.m. the next morning, and his first words were, "I am a conscientious objector." We immediately submitted a request for a determination of his conscientious objection status and a request that he be released from the military service. These actions were taken quietly, without publicity and without fanfare. My objective was to have David released from the service, not garner national attention and not fuel the fires of revolt against the Vietnam conflict. David's application cited language from each of three latest United States Supreme Court cases. His request for conscientious objector status and release from the Army was submitted at 1:30 p.m., stopping his re-assignment to Vietnam.

His application was processed quickly through the chain of command at Fort Lewis. Each commander denied the request without knowing the legal criteria, and none of these commanders actually interviewed David. The application was submitted to US Army Headquarters in Washington. Pending final action on his application, he was assigned to inspect all of the latrines in every building and every home on base at Fort Lewis and to render a report weekly.

While his application was pending, David and I became good friends. I admired the depth of his faith, his appetite for learning and his shear joy in doing what he felt was right. Thankfully, the Department of Army granted his request, and he was released from the military without a criminal trial for refusing orders of a senior officer and without having to serve in a combat role in Vietnam. In the process, his parents disowned him and his fiancé terminated their wedding plans. David returned to Germany to teach English at an orphanage in West Berlin. A year later, when Claudia and I journeyed to West Berlin on leave, we renewed our friendship with David. Unfortunately, I have not seen him since 1971.

Our year at Fort Lewis was also filled with fun and friendships. Our neighbors across the street, Judy and Gary Perola, came over one night with a Seattle newspaper, indicating that miniature poodles were for sale. There was a for sale notice about Afghan puppies also. Claudia said she had always wanted an Afghan hound. I had never heard of them or seen one. The four of us drove to Seattle that night and looked at miniature poodle puppies.

Afghan puppies are the ugliest, clumsiest looking animals I had ever seen. The lady selling the puppies lived in a frame house with a full basement. Her two female adults had given birth to twelve puppies, only two of which remained unsold. Chemay was four months old at the time and she had never been outside. Claudia fell in love with Chemay. However, we left Seattle without purchasing her.

The following day was Claudia's birthday. I went home for lunch at noon, and all Claudia could talk about was the puppy we saw the night before. I told her that somebody had already bought it. At the end of lunch, I told her that I was the one that had bought Chemay. I told her that if she wanted to go pick her up that afternoon, she could do so. She drove to Seattle by herself in our new Oldsmobile Cutlass Supreme. She returned later that afternoon with this scrawny, ugly, awkward four-month-old Afghan puppy. Chemay had never been outside before that car ride. She messed all over the car on the way back from Seattle. It was a major adventure to clean up the car, but Claudia was happy, and that was what I wanted.

Chemay was an unusual dog. The first night she was in our house, we showed her the papers at the back door. For the next three months, that is where she went to the bathroom. I would take her for long walks, sometimes for more than an hour, and immediately upon returning to the house, she would mess on the papers. Chemay only liked to chew on left shoes. Claudia had fifty or sixty pairs of shoes when we got married. It did not take Chemay long to find them boxed in the closet. Chemay grew into a beautiful dog that ran with grace and elegance and provided us much joy.

Shortly after acquiring Chemay, Claudia and I went to the White Mountain pass for skiing. We rode an Army bus four hours to get to the mountain by mid-morning and skied the rest of the day. I had never skied before. I took no lessons, found it incredibly difficult and spent most of my time lying in snow banks unable to get up.

About three months after arriving at Fort Lewis, I received a telephone call from CPT Friedenberger. "I understand you want to go to Europe." COL York had obviously relayed my request to the career management office. John asked where I wanted to go and what I wanted to do. I told him that I wanted to go to the largest general court-martial jurisdiction in Germany, and I would like to take the three-week military procurement law course en route. In early December 1969, I received orders consistent with my request.

In April 1969 I was notified that I was to be the sponsor for a new captain reporting for duty at Fort Lewis later that month. I was told that Tom Dolan was the son of a New York City policeman and that he and his wife, Barbara, would be arriving in about three weeks. My idea of people from New York City was clearly as wrong as his vision of what people from Oklahoma would be like. Barbara and Tom arrived in the afternoon on Friday, driving a station wagon with a canoe strapped to the top. They had driven from New York through Minnesota and Wisconsin to arrive at Fort Lewis, camping along the way, in the middle of winter. We became instant friends. As his sponsor, my duties were to show Tom around Fort Lewis. Claudia was responsible for showing Barbara the ropes.

Almost immediately after arriving, Tom and Barbara purchased a German Shephard puppy, Thorn. During the July 4th weekend in 1969, the Slickers and the Dolans, along with their dogs, journeyed to the Olympic peninsula to fish and camp out. Unfortunately, it rained the entire weekend. The dogs were sopping wet, they smelled, the girls stayed in the tent, and Tom and I caught no fish. The girls hated it. We all hated it, but we had an adventure we still talk about.

In late August 1969, to celebrate COL Lee's 30th wedding anniversary, a salmon fishing trip was organized for the entire JAGC office. Most of the fifteen lawyers and their wives (excluding COL Lee's wife) decided to go. We left at 3:30 a.m. for West Port, approximately 100 miles south of Fort Lewis. After eating a scrumptious breakfast of bacon, sausage, eggs, biscuits and potatoes, we boarded our chartered fishing boat at 6:30 a.m. and left the harbor with approximately 500 other fishing boats to travel approximately twenty miles off the Washington coast to fish for salmon. In the process, most of us got totally sick, and some of us spent most of the day below deck turning various shades of green.

We caught numerous sea bass and our boat's limit of salmon. Fresh salmon cooked over a barbeque grill with lemon and butter became my favorite meal. COL Lee bought a washer and dryer for his wife's wedding anniversary. He had a great time fishing.

I was asked to travel to Vancouver, British Columbia, to arrange the release of an AWOL American soldier from Oklahoma, who had stolen and used credit cards and gone on a buying spree all the way to Canada, charging more than the limit on the stolen credit card. Because he was a US Army soldier, I was able to obtain his release from Canadian custody and return him to the Army. In the process, Claudia and I got to spend a tremendously enjoyable day in Vancouver, an unbelievably beautiful city surrounded by mountains on three sides and by the Puget Sound on the west.

Departing Fort Lewis was an adventure. In late November, Claudia miscarried and was advised not to travel by car on our way home to Kansas for Christmas before our departure for Germany. So Claudia flew home, and Chemay and I drove the Cutlass from Fort Lewis to Pratt, KS. After white-gloving the house, Chemay and I departed Fort Lewis one snowy December afternoon. By the time we reached Portland, OR a massive snowstorm was in progress.

We drove four hours after Portland and finally stopped in a small Oregon town off the freeway. I did not know whether motels would permit dogs, so I got a room on the ground floor and did not tell the hotel proprietor about Chemay. After settling in, we went for a brief walk. My calm, beautiful, graceful dog suddenly hit a brace. She froze in her tracks and she started growling, which I had never heard her do. Chemay was looking at a snowman with a carrot nose, a black top hat and a red scarf. She would not go close to that snowman.

The following day Chemay and I drove 300 or 400 miles in a blinding snow storm. We drove until I was exhausted. I finally pulled off of the interstate and checked into a small four-cottage motel. There were several feet of snow on the ground surrounding our little cabin, which had two double beds and was a warm place to stay. Since both Chemay and I were hungry, we journeyed to the only restaurant in this small community. It was a truck stop near the interstate. Chemay and I walked into this restaurant, and I ordered two orders of fries and two cheeseburgers. I can only imagine what they must have thought of me.

The next day we drove from Idaho to Denver, CO. In the process, I had a flat tire in western Wyoming. I had to unload the entire trunk to get the spare out with temperatures near zero and a 30 mph wind blowing unchecked across this largely uninhabited wasteland. Chemay and I limped into Cheyenne late in the afternoon. I got the tire fixed, and we headed for Denver. Again, I was exhausted. Several miles outside of Denver, I was determined to stop at the first hotel I came to in the Denver area. I arrived at a Holiday Inn fifteen miles outside of Denver about 9 p.m. that Friday evening. I took a room in the hotel away from the highway on the first floor. After showering, I sat on the bed in my under shorts and called Claudia.

During the telephone call, Chemay had to go to the bathroom. I tied her rope on her collar, tied the rope to the door and let her out. About three minutes later, I heard this terrible yelp. She had pulled the rope under the tire of a car parked in the parking lot and could not get loose. I reached over and pulled the rope away from the tire, and Chemay jerked pulling the hotel door closed. There I stood, dressed only in my under shorts in six degree temperature with snow falling profusely all around, holding an Afghan hound on a rope. My only choice was to walk into the lobby and get a key for the room.

The lobby was filled with people in tuxedos and formal gowns, preparing to enter the ballroom for a formal Christmas party. I do not know what they thought about the streeker with the Afghan, but the people behind the desk quickly got me the hell out of the lobby and into my room. Claudia was still on the phone when I returned.

We had planned to take Chemay with us to Germany. I had her papers translated into German, and I purchased a large container for her shipment in the hull of the aircraft. I had been told the cost was approximately $1 per pound for the weight of the dog and her create or approximately $75. Instead, the cost was $1.52 per pound, determined by multiplying the average displacement weight in the aircraft of the massive crate. Instead of $75, it was going to cost almost $400 for us to ship Chemay to Germany. I simply did not have the money. Consequently, we left Chemay with Bernard and Barbara Nordling, my aunt and uncle in western Kansas. Claudia and I journeyed to Germany without Chemay. We were, nevertheless, able to take Claudia's cat, Boo Boo.

Germany
1970-72

We arrived in Worms, Germany, on the banks of the Rhine River on a cold gray day in early February 1970. Boo Boo struggled but survived the cold crossing of the Atlantic. We soon settled into the one bedroom bachelor officers quarters suite at the main headquarters of the Theater Army Support Command Headquarters (TASCOM). We were ready to begin an adventure which was to last more than thirty-two months.

TASCOM was the major support and logistics command for all of US Army Europe and was the largest general court-martial jurisdiction in Europe with troops scattered all over Western Europe. Because automatic review of special court-martial cases was required, the TASCOM JAGC office also got assigned to try all of the cases arising within US Army Europe. These troops were in Northern Africa, Turkey, Greece, France, Belgium and in other far flung areas in the region.

My first Monday afternoon in the office was truly a command performance. I had never even seen a two star general before, but I received a request to report to Major General W. W. Vaughn's office at 3:00 p.m. As Commanding General, he required that every new officer in the command meet and be welcomed by him personally. I still remember being incredibly impressed with him. He seemed to me to be the personification of the US Army: tall, distinguished, warm and friendly. I left there believing that I would do anything this man asked me to do, not because I had to but because I wanted to please him.

One of his aides was 1LT Jerry Compton. Jerry and Marsha became our best friends. One evening on a Rhine River cruise, Jerry, the general and I drank far too much wine and learned far too much about the general's escapades while he was a cadet at West Point. One of Jerry's favorite sayings was, "Well, press my shorts." We needed more than this homespun humor to get out of bed the next day.

My first official act in the TASCOM JAGC office was to request leave to go skiing two months after we arrived in Germany. I look back now and cannot believe that I had the nerve to do that, but the ski trip was memorable. We drove in our new red Opel GT, a miniature Corvette look-alike, from Worms to Berchesgaden, in the Southeastern corner of the German Bavarian Alps. Several times we were passed by Volkswagen bugs going more than 100 miles an hour on the Autobahn. I kept my speed down to 85 mph. To the Germans, driving is not a means to get from point A to point B. Driving is an adventure, a sport, where the goal is to go as fast as possible with reckless abandon and utter disregard for anyone's safety, even their own.

We stayed in an exquisite hotel used by the SS and senior NAZI officials during World War II, before the US Army liberated it. The hotel was located less than two kilometers from Eagle's Nest, where Hitler wrote *Mien Kampf.* The mountains were unbelievably beautiful, and the local culture defied even the remotest possibility of the events that lead to the US Army's presence in Germany. The people were joyous and friendly, happy and always ready to drink beer and party. I still do not understand how these fun loving people could permit a Hitler to terrorize their lives and the safety of the whole world.

We were able to take ski lessons every day for five days, rent our equipment, eat on the slopes and travel back and forth from skiing to the hotel, all for $2 a day. The hotel room was also $2 a day. We spent a total of less than $200 that week, and we purchased a beautiful painting in a gold frame by Albert Bierstadt for $100. The painting was later contributed to Holland Hall Preparatory School in Tulsa at a fair market value of more than $10,000. What an adventure! On the last day of skiing, our group of five got to participate in slalom races down the mountain. Of course, Claudia won out of three women in her race. I struggled to be third out of two. I fell in exactly the same place on both runs down the mountain. It was still fun.

Several months later, LTG Vaughn was promoted and was replaced by LTG Eifler as TASCOM Commander. General Eifler was the exact opposite of his predecessor. General Eifler was short, probably 5'6" in height. He parted his short hair down the middle of his head. He was a stern, all business, almost scary little man who showed little warmth or weakness. He was not interested in being liked. He preferred being feared. Even before he took command at TASCOM, it was reported that he fired several full colonels in the command, resulting in the disruption of their families and the lives of many others.

I also remember that I would do anything asked of me by this man, not because I loved him or respected him, but because I, along with most others, feared his power over me. He had the power to change my life dramatically. The difference between these two highly successful leaders made a real impression on me. Both fear and respect can be effective. I choose the latter. I learned firsthand that honey attracts more bees than vinegar; that effective results can be achieved through example, respect and charisma, even though fear can also be an effective motivator.

The TASCOM JAGC office was staffed by seventeen Army lawyers and two German civilian lawyers when I reported for duty. I was the youngest of five captains. There were majors, lieutenant colonels and two full colonels. COL Gerald W. Davis, a distinguished officer and a terrific lawyer, was the boss. I was assigned initially as a defense lawyer in the Military Justice Division. I defended at trial a wide variety of cases arising in far flung sites in France, Belgium and Germany. Within a few months, most of the officers in the office when I arrived had rotated out of Germany or out of the service, leaving me as Chief of Military Justice, a senior lieutenant colonel slot and the third senior officer in the office. Because of this unique situation, during the last half of my time in Germany, I got to try the cases that were most interesting.

There were angels all around me during this exciting time, especially since I was in the comfort of Germany, while many of my friends and over 650,000 US troops were fighting an endless fight in Vietnam. My angels kept me safe, though not without some amusing and interesting war stories to tell. My war stories were fought in the courtroom, not on the battlefield. Thank God!

Claudia and I made great friends while we were in the Army in Germany. Some of those friends included Jerry and Marsha Compton. Jerry left the service about one year after we arrived, but he remained in Germany as a civil service employee. Corky and Armeda Messinger were also great friends. Corky, like Jerry, was a general's aide. Larry and Susan Ritner were our best friends. Larry was a civilian in charge of the wood working and other craft shops at Worms. He was extremely helpful, because off-base housing consisted of apartments with only walls, no cabinets or closets, even in the kitchen. I ended up building closets and cabinets for our apartment off-base, and Larry and Susan helped enormously in this effort.

Paul and Debbie Spitzberg were also close friends. Debbie was a gorgeous blonde with long straight hair. Paul was a young, cocky Jewish banker in charge of the American Express Bank at Worms. He was happy, friendly, knew everybody and wanted to be everybody's friend. He and I both loved baseball and enjoyed umpiring together. In one championship game, I was umpiring behind the plate, and

Paul was umpiring at third base, so that he would not have to make any crucial calls that would cause people to be upset with him. Late in the game, with the Chief of Staff's son hitting and with his team behind, a ball was hit for what looked like a home run. However, the general's son missed third base as he came home. I saw that he missed third base. Paul saw that he missed third base, and so did the coach on the opposing team. An appeal was made, and the general's son was called out. The game was over, and all hell broke loose. Poor Paul! He made the correct call, but he also made some very powerful enemies in the process.

We frequently took weekend trips to France, Holland and Switzerland. We also went on Rhine River cruises or trips into the wine country in Germany. On one eventful trip, Debbie, Paul, Claudia and I decided at noon to drive to France for dinner. We had heard about a wonderful five star restaurant in a small French village called Liverdun. It was approximately 100 miles from Worms. On the way we stopped to buy wine, cheese and French bread. We then drove into this farming community that looked like something out of medieval times. Ox drawn carts were on the cobblestone streets. The little community could not have had more than 500 or 600 inhabitants. In this town, however, there was an unbelievable restaurant, one of only a few five star restaurants in all of France. We had the most scrumptious meal I have ever eaten and retired to a small bedroom upstairs from the restaurant with fresh flowers and perfume filling the air. Debbie made a big hit with all of the French men.

On another weekend, Claudia and I and our Worms friends went to Baden Baden to gamble and enjoy the spas. Baden Baden was approximately 100 miles south of Worms in the Black Forest. It was a picturesque setting. On another occasion, we took the all-night train from Frankfurt to Berlin, where we met David Bean, my former conscientious objector client from Fort Lewis who was teaching English in a small German orphanage in West Berlin. We traveled to Amsterdam during the tulip festival, where we visited the famous Dutch painting museums, saw the International Court at The Hague and enjoyed the friendliness of the Dutch people. We spent a weekend in London going to plays and shopping at Harrod's.

We drove to Paris one weekend where we met John Jones, my high school friend, who was living in Paris auditing American Express banks in that region. We also met John in Rome during the July 4th weekend. The hotel workers were on strike, so almost all the other workers went on strike too. While inconvenient, that did not keep us from seeing the great sites in Rome, including the Vatican. We even saw the Pope give a special blessing to American service men and women. We also traveled to Munich, Stuttgart, Heidelberg and Salzburg. We traveled throughout the German wine country. We went to Switzerland and Rome and Florence. In short, we had a glorious experience, both personally and professionally.

Truth is Not a Defense

One of my first assignments was to prosecute a special court-martial case in an air defense artillery unit four kilometers away from the East German border in northeastern Germany. The installation was surrounded by razor wire, German shepherd dogs paroled the perimeter and numerous US missiles were pointed east to Moscow. In 1970, our relations with the Soviet Union were strained. The accused was a Specialist-4 college graduate assigned to the military hospital administration staff. The charge was disrespect of a senior officer by saying that the LTC in charge of administration was "stupid." The LTC who complained was a native of Puerto Rico, a career US Army officer with more than twenty five years in service. Despite his lengthy service, his English was broken. It was difficult to understand him. Stupid is as stupid does. The defense was that the accused made a comment that a particular policy was stupid, not that the LTC was stupid. There was no denial that the accused said the word stupid. The only issue was in what context.

The trial judge was a good friend of mine, a black JAGC captain with whom I had previously tried numerous cases. My task was to prosecute the case, get a conviction and return back to Worms. There were only two witnesses in the case. I called the LTC, who stated that he heard the accused say that the Colonel was stupid. The defendant testified that he never called the LTC stupid, but he admitted that he made an off-handed comment about a particular policy that he though was stupid. His testimony was that the policy was stupid, not the LTC. My final argument consisted of six words: "Truth is not a defense to disrespect." My friend, the black trial judge, was furious with me. He almost held me in contempt, because my reference clearly indicated that I thought the LTC was stupid, if for no other reason than for bringing such a stupid charge. I got a conviction. The accused was sentenced to two months confinement and reduced in grade to Private E-1.

Jason Reed

Jason Reed was one of McNamara's special 100,000 troops. During Vietnam, Secretary of Defense Robert McNamara instituted a policy that permitted more than 100,000 men with low IQ's and low test scores to enlist in military service. Many of those soldiers later got in trouble with the justice system, simply because they did not understand what was at stake. Jason Reed was one of those. Jason Reed was a Private E-2 when I first met him. His duty was to assist the local Red Cross office in maintaining proper files in the Red Cross office. The civilian who ran the office had just purchased a new Mercedes 250 and was scheduled to be on leave over the weekend. He often asked Jason to do favors for him personally. On this day, he pitched Jason the keys to his new Mercedes and told Jason to wash and wax the car and return it to him on Monday. Jason did in fact wash and wax the car, but he also drove it 50 miles north of Worms to an NCO club Saturday night. Upon returning, he was involved in an accident that resulted in several thousand dollars of damage to the new Mercedes. Jason was charged with automobile theft. I was assigned to defend him. I argued that there was no wrongful taking, since Jason was given the keys to the car by owner. He was acquitted, much to the dismay and consternation of the Red Cross administrator.

Jason always seemed to be in trouble. He was about 6'2", very friendly and handsome, but clearly one with low wattage. He had a friend who was very bright and very "street smart." The two of them hung around the headquarters commandant's office a lot. They ran errands and did odd jobs for him. Two weeks before a scheduled visit by the Commanding General, United States Army Europe, the HQ commandant "suggested" to Jason and his friend that it would be nice if the headquarters could be cleaned up for the General's visit. Jason and his friend allegedly stole, that is, mysteriously acquired, 500 gallons of paint from an Army warehouse, which was then used to freshen up the place for the General's visit. No one was ever prosecuted for this little misadventure.

Jason's friend played the drums in a country and western band. A warrant officer turned captain was the lead male singer and lead guitar player. The captain's wife was the female vocalist. There were two staff sergeants who also played the guitar in this band. Jason would go along to carry all of the equipment and do other tasks that no one else wanted to do. During intermission, Jason banged on the drums. He did not know how to play the drums, but he beat on them anyway. Everybody thought it was funny. Some time later that evening Jason made a comment which the captain took as an offensive comment toward the captain's wife. The two sergeants decided to teach Jason a lesson. While Jason and his friend were driving back to Worms, the two sergeants pulled their car over, hauled Jason out of his car and beat the hell out of him.

Instead of taking Jason to the hospital, Jason's friend decided that the two sergeants should take Jason to the hospital. So he went to his quarters, got his .22 pistol, went to the two sergeants' homes and at gunpoint directed them to take Jason to the hospital. When one of the sergeants seemed reluctant, Jason's friend put a bullet about three inches over the reluctant sergeant's right ear. Jason's friend was an expert shot with a pistol. He could hit the eye out of a rabbit running at full speed at 300 yards. He did not attempt to kill the sergeant, just to scare him. So much for country justice!

Jason's friend was charged with attempted murder, two counts of kidnapping, carrying a concealed a weapon and other assorted charges. I was assigned to defend him in general court. Four of the charges had maximum punishments of life imprisonment. The prosecution called the two sergeants who were guitar players as the only government witnesses. I called the captain, his wife and Jason's friend as my only witnesses. Jason's friend was convicted of reckless endangerment and given a sentence of three months in confinement and reduced to the grade of private E-1. He was not discharged from the service. He was acquitted on all other charges. The captain and the two sergeants were assigned out of the command. The charges were perhaps technically correct but grossly overstated under the circumstances. Jason's friend was very lucky.

Melvin Belli

Melvin Belli was a famous, wealthy and very prestigious criminal defense lawyer whose offices were in San Francisco. On certain occasions, Mr. Belli would travel to Europe to defend soldiers charged with serious offenses. On one occasion, he defended a staff sergeant charged with raping an eighteen-year-old German girl. A friend of mine was prosecuting, so I asked to observe the trial.

The victim's testimony was very strong, though there were no corroborating witnesses. I sat right behind Mr. Belli during his cross-examination. He inquired in a very haphazard approach about the girl's background, her boyfriends, her experience sexually, the events of the night in question and other related topics. At one point, he asked her if she had a doctor. She responded that she did. He then asked for the doctor's name. Several minutes later he picked up a piece of paper the size of a prescription paper, but which was in fact blank. He asked if she had received a prescription for contraceptives. In 1971, unmarried women who used contraceptive devices were thought to be promiscuous. The girl responded that she had just recently obtained a prescription for contraceptive pills. Mr. Belli succeeded in a very non-threatening way to cast doubt over the victim's moral character by implying the victim was promiscuous. The result was an acquittal. I think the girl was in fact raped, but unfortunately character of the victim in a rape case is crucial.

LTC Frank Acosta

LTC Frank Acosta was a highly-decorated Vietnam veteran, having served three tours in Vietnam and having been the helicopter pilot for numerous general grade officers, including four star General Westmoreland, US Commander in Vietnam. He had earned three Silver Star awards for valor, numerous Bronze Stars for valor and other combat awards. After more than twenty-three years in the Army, LTC Acosta was assigned as the security officer for the super secret cryptographic photography repository at TASCOM headquarters, which contained photographs taken from U-2 missions surreptitiously flown over the USSR.

LTC Acosta was definitely a lady's man. He had girlfriends everywhere, from Munich to Frankfurt. One of his girlfriends was the Chief of Staff's secretary with whom LTC Acosta co-habited several nights a week. The secretary often took his uniforms to be laundered. On one occasion, while cleaning out his pockets, she discovered a marriage license in which LTC Acosta had married the nineteen-year-old daughter of the mayor of a small German town outside Worms, Germany. She was shocked and scorned. Hell hath no fury like the scorn of a rebuffed woman. She immediately brought the marriage license to the attention of the Commanding General, who commenced an investigation and discovered that LTC Acosta had in fact married the young woman in question, but LTC Acosta was already married to a woman living in California with whom he had four children. In an overseas area, every service man must get permission from all the commanders in his chain of command to marry a foreign national, because the foreign national becomes a dependent of the United States government by reason of the marriage. An application for permission to get married is required to be submitted through the chain of command. The application requires each commander's approval and several parts of the application must to be signed and notarized. LTC Acosta simply forged the signatures of officers purporting to act as notaries for the acknowledgments contained in the application. LTC Acosta was charged with bigamy and several counts of forgery. I was assigned to prosecute the case.

The forgery charges were relatively easy. There were two hand-writing experts in US Army Europe at the time, each of whom examined the handwriting on six separate documents and opined conclusively that LTC Acosta had in fact written the signatures on these documents. I had each handwriting expert prepare approximately 150 large photographs to illustrate how he reached his conclusive opinion.

The bigamy charge was more difficult. I had to prove that LTC Acosta had gotten married at a time when he was married to a person who was then still living. I had to prove that LTC Acosta's wife in California was alive and that they had not divorced. Because he was supporting her financially, she refused to testify. Both of them were Catholics, and neither of them believed in divorce. By using official records, I determined where LTC Acosta had been stationed over his entire military career; and I obtained official records from the county clerks in each county adjacent to every duty station where he was assigned to the effect that no divorce action had been filed involving LTC Acosta. I also used official records to confirm payments each month from LTC Acosta to his wife in California, and I showed that the checks payable to Mrs. Frank Acosta were cashed by a person at the location where his first wife resided. Finally, I had two detectives in San Francisco go to Mrs. Acosta's home, knock on the door and ask if she was Mrs. Frank Acosta. The hearsay exclusion raised serious and difficult questions with respect to each of these efforts to prove bigamy.

LTC Acosta knew many general grade and senior field grade officers. Prior to trial he requested that twenty three character witnesses be produced, eight of whom were general grade officers and three of whom were four-star generals. My task was to determine whether these men knew LTC Acosta and whether arrangements could be made for them to attend the trial. My general ordered me to request that more than half of the officers on the defense list be produced as defense witnesses. This required me to make phone calls all over the world, including talking to one full colonel who was engaged in hostile action in Vietnam at the time of my phone call and who thought I was crazy requesting that he leave the firefight and come to Germany to testify as a defense character witness for "that old son of a bitch." My general determined that approximately half of the character witnesses were not necessary for LTC Acosta's defense.

Instead of making a request that only those persons who were denied attendance by my general as a character witness, the defense renewed its request in a pre-trial hearing that all twenty three persons be ordered to appear as a defense witness. The judge in a pre-trial conference determined that none of the witnesses, including the generals, were required to attend. At that same pre-trial conference, the judge determined that the forgery charges, which I had nailed with absolute proof, were improper, ruling that the documents, even if signed by LTC Acosta, were not of the character or type that could be forged under the applicable military forgery law. I was required to go to trial with one count of bigamy and one count of conduct unbecoming of an officer.

LTC Acosta pled not guilty, and each of my official records from the various county clerks was admitted over objection that they violated the hearsay rule. Two criminal investigators in San Francisco went to the home of Mrs. Frank Acosta. When the door was answered, they asked if the person answering the door was Mrs. Frank Acosta. Their testimony was also admitted into evidence over hearsay objections. I got a conviction on the bigamy charge and on the conduct unbecoming of an officer charge, solely using documents. After the trial, LTC Acosta came up and shook my hand and told me what a great job I had done and told me that the next time he had problems, he would ask for me as his defense counsel. The court fined LTC Acosta $20,000 but did not remove him from the service.

Turkish Hashish

One of my funniest cases involved a charge that never went to trial. A staff sergeant drew the short straw to take a weekend pass to Turkey to purchase $22,000 of Turkish hashish. At the time, Turkish hashish was thought to be the highest grade of marijuana available. It was typically sold in blocks about the size of a small cigarette package. The sergeant returned to Germany from Turkey carrying two suitcases filled with over one hundred blocks of what everyone thought was Turkish hashish. The sergeant was immediately placed in pre-trial custody, and the contraband was submitted to the criminal investigation chemistry lab to confirm its authenticity. The sergeant was charged with possession of illegal substances with the intent to distribute.

Two weeks later, I got a call from the head chemist at the Criminal Investigation Detachment lab. We had established an elaborate chain of custody to make sure that the contraband brought into Germany by this soldier was the exact same material that was tested and admitted into evidence at trial. Our elaborate efforts were unnecessary. The chemist confirmed that the contraband looked like Turkish hashish and smelled like Turkish hashish but was in fact camel shit. I informed COL Davis, who later informed Commanding General Eifler. The sergeant was either guilty of fraud, if he knew the briquettes in his suitcases were not hashish, or he was guilty of attempted possession of a controlled substance with the intent to distribute. He had a perfect defense to the criminal charges: "I knew it was camel shit." There is no law that makes it criminal to attempt to possess camel shit, even though other common law crimes were accompanied by statutes which prohibited attempts to commit such crimes. I recommended returning the sergeant to his unit. The "evidence" was destroyed.

Judge School

One of the most interesting experiences I had was attending judge school for two weeks in Charlottesville, VA. Fifty or sixty lawyers were trained to act like, talk like and decide like a special court-martial judge. The last day of judge school involved a "sentencing institute," in which we were divided up into small groups. We were given several different factual problems, told that the accused had been convicted of a specific offense, informed what the maximum punishment was and asked to decide the sentence. In my group there were two Navy lieutenants, one Marine captain, one Air Force captain and two Army captains, including me. The other Army captain and one of the Navy officers had served in Vietnam.

Even though we were about the same age with the same level of education and approximately the same time in the military, our backgrounds and our approaches to sentencing varied widely. The Marine officer and the two Navy lawyers were very harsh. I was the most lenient in cases not involving physical injury to others. Hearing each officer describe the reasons for the sentence he imposed was tremendously informative to me. As a policy matter, our society, not just the military, is struggling with the wide disparity in sentencing for the same offense.

Because I was the senior captain in the Military Justice Division at TASCOM, COL Davis did not let me hear too many cases as a judge. He needed me to process the cases in the office. I remember two specific cases in which I did serve as judge. One involved a virtual race riot that took place in Mannheim, Germany, in which several white soldiers and several black solders engaged in a brawl in the company mess hall. Only the black soldiers were prosecuted. I listened to the evidence and entered not guilty findings with respect to each of the black accused. That was not a popular result, but it was the correct result. Racial tensions subsided. The white witnesses told exactly the same story with the same words. I simply did not believe them. A riot does not produce uniformity in testimony. The very nature of the event was mass confusion, so uniform testimony had to raise suspicions as to veracity.

The other cased involved a larceny. It took the command seventy-five days to bring the case to trial, while the accused was in pre-trial custody. I granted a motion to dismiss the charges on speedy trial grounds, after considering testimony from several witnesses and after considering the simple nature of the charges. Again, my decision was not popular but it was correct.

In most special court-martial cases, the military judge is a major or a senior captain who wears his military uniform while hearing the case. At the general court-martial level, the trial judges, generally full colonels, often wear a black robe, though they were not required to do so. As a special court martial judge, it was absolutely unheard of for the trial judge to wear a black robe. I borrowed a robe from the church choir in Worms.

I wore a robe while judging every case I tried as a judge. As a result, the tensions in the court room were significantly reduced when compared to a trial where the judge wears an officer's uniform. The accused regarded the judge wearing a robe with more respect.

I found the experience of judging both exhilarating and very different from being a trial lawyer. As a trial lawyer, I was given one side of a case to zealously argue. My whole focus as a prosecutor was to prove my case and get justice for the victim. My focus as a defense counsel was to present reasonable doubt to secure an acquittal. As an advocate for either side, I was never called upon to determine the truth, veracity or credibility of the evidence. As a trial judge, determining the veracity of the witnesses and weighing their credibility is the primary function. I took each task seriously, whether I was a trial advocate or the ultimate decider of facts. I found the judge duty difficult but intellectually very challenging.

Pin Cushion Murder

The last three cases I prosecuted in the Army involved a murder case, an aggravated knife-point rape case and a vehicular homicide case. The murder case and the rape case occurred on the same evening approximately one mile from each other at Kaiserslautern, about sixty miles west of Worms.

In the murder case, a relatively young black soldier was prosecuted for first degree murder after he inflicted 42 knife wounds in a white soldier's back. The victim's back looked like a pin cushion. There were two separate crime scenes separated by approximately 400 yards. At the first crime scene, there was a small pool of blood where the initial knife attack took place. Between that crime scene and the place where the body was discovered, there was a trail of blood and a large pool of blood under the victim where he died. The evidence revealed that the victim made a homosexual proposition to the defendant, and the knife attack represented the defendant's response. I won a conviction and a twenty-five year sentence in that case. So much for gays in the military!

71

Rape of a School Teacher

The rape case involved a black staff sergeant accused of raping a beautiful white American school teacher at knife point. Her apartment was located on the second floor of the same building in which the military police office was located on the first floor. She lived alone. There was no broken lock on the door way, there were no deadbolt locks, no chains installed and no peepholes in the door to determine who was outside. After the rape, the victim offered the accused a cup of coffee, which he accepted and then left her apartment. She immediately took a bath before reporting to the rape crisis clinic. With the aid of a police artist, she drew a fairly accurate picture of the accused, and his fingerprints were located on the coffee cup from which he drank coffee after the rape.

The wife of the accused tried to give her husband an alibi, but the wife's testimony on cross-examination did not hold up, and the accused's testimony was garbled and unreliable after extensive cross-examination. He denied that he was ever in the victim's apartment, which we knew was not true, given the fingerprints found at the scene. The jury convicted the defendant and imposed a ten-year sentence, which was reduced by my general to three years. Ironically, a black man raped a white woman in Dallas, TX, at approximately the same time as my rape case occurred. The jury convicted that black rapist and sentenced him to 6,000 years in jail. That rape occurred through physical force but without the benefit of a knife. Neither woman was physically harmed, beaten up or otherwise injured physically, except for her violation through the rape. I found the sentencing discrepancy incredibly difficult to understand and hard to reconcile from the point of view of justice.

The Lying Son of a Bitch Case

The last criminal case I prosecuted involved the death of the bartender at the officers' club in Asmara, Ethiopia. The victim was riding his bike home from work about midnight when he was struck from the rear by a car driven by a US Army sergeant. The victim was killed instantly. The sergeant left the scene of the crime without stopping to help.

Asmara is located on the northern high plateau of Ethiopia, near the Red Sea. It is one of the best satellite tracking locations in the world. The US had approximately 600 troops stationed in Asmara, primarily to operate, maintain and monitor information obtained through several huge satellite dishes there and to provide security for those dishes.

There is a status of forces agreement between the US government and each foreign government when US troops are present in a foreign jurisdiction. This agreement contains, among other things, provisions relating to primary and secondary jurisdiction in criminal cases. Generally, the United States prefers to prosecute its own soldiers for alleged criminal offenses committed on foreign soil, whether those offenses occurred on or off the US military base and whether or not the crime involved foreign nationals or other soldiers. My case involved a vehicular manslaughter of a foreign national at a location off the military installation. The US Army asserted primary jurisdiction, and the Ethiopian government deferred.

US constitutional law and federal criminal law principles apply in criminal trials in the military. The law of search and seizure under the Fourth Amendment to the US Constitution, as applied in federal district courts in the US, is essentially the same search and seizure law used in US military courts, wherever the trial occurs. Unless the search or seizure is incident to a lawful arrest, the law requires that probable cause support a search warrant in order for any search and seizure to be valid and for the evidence obtained to be admissible at trial. Unless the search and seizure are valid, evidence obtained is inadmissible at trial as the "fruit of a poisonous tree." In the military, the commanding officer makes the determination of probable cause, which a magistrate or trial judge would make in the civilian context. If evidence of a crime is in "plain view," then admission of that evidence and any evidence which flows from that plain view seizure would also be admissible at trial, even in the absence of a search warrant.

In my case, the car did not belong to the sergeant who was driving it at the time of the accident, but instead belonged to one of his friends. The friend lived off the military installation behind ten foot walls. In order for the car to be in "plain view," someone had to look over the walls. When doing so, the right front light of the car in the garage was visible from outside the fence and was broken. The bumper was dented in, and the victim's blood was on the bumper of the car. Whether the car was in "plain view" or not was the legal issue that intrigued me the most about this case. If the arrest of the sergeant driving the car occurred pursuant to an illegal search of his friend's residence, the arrest would not have been valid, and the evidence about the condition of the car would not be admissible at trial. If the physical evidence relating to the car was not in "plain view," then a search warrant was required before the enforcement personnel could lawfully enter upon the premises of the friend where the car was parked. For the search warrant to be valid, probable cause would be required. There was no search warrant in this case.

The accused was charged with involuntary manslaughter, leaving the scene of the accident involving personal injury and conduct unbecoming of a noncommissioned officer. The accused claimed that he was so drunk that night that he did not have any recollection of anything that occurred, and therefore he could not plead guilty to leaving the scene of the accident, since he did not know he was in an accident. The accused was sent from Asmara, Ethiopia, to Frankfurt,

Germany, for a week-long psychiatric examination by a psychiatrist in the Army hospital in Frankfurt. The psychiatrist rendered a report that stated in general that blackouts and amnesia often occur as a result of long periods of alcoholic binging. The accused could be correct in stating the he suffered from alcoholic amnesia. Therefore, the defense argued that the accused could not be guilty of the specific intent crime of leaving the scene of an accident involving personal injury, since the accused was so intoxicated that he did not even know that he had been involved in an accident.

When I boarded the plane in Frankfurt for my trip to Asmara, Ethiopia, to prosecute this case, my assigned seat was next to a major in the United States Army. The major was the primary defense witness in the case I was about to prosecute. Our flight took us to Rome and then to Asmara. The two flights lasted approximately seven hours. The psychiatrist was two weeks away from leaving the Army and returning to Washington, DC, to open a psychiatric practice there. He had never testified in a criminal case, and he had never observed a military court-martial. He was very interested in the process and asked me many questions about the accused in this case. Each time he mentioned his "patient," I responded by saying that I was not permitted to talk about the case, but that his patient was a "lying son of a bitch." Upon arriving in Asmara, the two of us found only two BOQ rooms available. These rooms are adjacent to each other and we shared a bathroom. It was ironic that the chief defense witness and the prosecuting attorney shared bathroom facilities for two days prior to and during the trial.

There were two JAGC officers stationed in Asmara, both of whom had graduated from Harvard and both of whom had interviewed the sergeant accused of this offense. Consequently, neither of these lawyers was available to prosecute this case. I had assigned the case to another lawyer in our office, but his wife was nine months pregnant when the case was set for trial, so I filled in to prosecute the case.

My case was relatively simply. If the arrest and the search incident to the arrest were valid and not in violation of the Fourth Amendment, or if the car was in plain view, then the arrest was valid and the seized at the scene was admissible. Once the trial judge admitted the evidence over defense objection, my case was relatively easy to prove.

The first defense witness was the psychiatrist. He testified beautifully that the accused could be suffering from alcoholic amnesia. My meager attempts to cross-examine the major proved totally fruitless. After he was dismissed from the witness stand, he requested the opportunity to watch the remaining trial. Military trials follow the "rule," which prohibits witnesses who have testified to watch the rest of the trial. The theory of the rule is that a witness may color or change or modify his or her testimony if given the opportunity to observe others testifying. The rule is invoked automatically. The psychiatrist requested the opportunity to watch the remaining portion of the trial, and the trial judge asked if I had any objection. I did not.

The only other defense witness was the accused. He testified that he was intoxicated on the evening in question, that did not know that he was driving a car, that he did know that his car was involved in an accident and that he did not know that he left the scene of an accident involving personal injury. He also testified that he had not had a drink during the 75 days since the accident. I rose to cross-examine. I literally had no hard evidence to refute his alcoholic amnesia, but I doubted his veracity when he testified that he had not had a drink in 75 days. I did know who his friends were. I believed that his friends would testify honestly that both they and he drank relatively constantly, since there was nothing else to do in Asmara other than to drink.

After some inconsequential cross-examination, I wrangled a judicial confession out of the accused when he admitted that he had lied when he testified that he had not drank alcohol since the accident. Since his credibility was tainted by this open court perjury, the remaining portion of his testimony became seriously suspect. He was convicted and sentenced to two months in confinement, with the jury recommending that his two months be suspended. This sentence was remarkably the same as the sentence given to Sen. Ted Kennedy after the Chappaquiddick incident, in which a woman riding in the Senator's car was killed. Senator Kennedy was drunk, he left the seen of the accident involving personal injury and he went to extraordinary lengths to cover it up. What is proper for a senator is proper for a sergeant!

As a footnote to the trial, while I was packing my bags to leave the courtroom, the military psychiatrist came up to me and said: "My patient is a lying son of a bitch!" He turned and walked out of the courtroom, and I have never seen him again.

There was only one flight out of Asmara, and it left at 1:00 p.m. the following day. I rose early in the morning and persuaded the defense counsel to drive me into the countryside, so I could see a little of Asmara. What I saw was shocking: unbelievable poverty. The average family income of Ethiopians at the time was approximately $400 a year. I saw first hand what starvation, disease and utter hopelessness was by looking in the blank enlarged eyes of the Ethiopian people who lived just outside of the city of Asmara.

This trial took place on the day before the first worldwide pilot's strike, which occurred to protest the lack of security at airports around the world and to protest the threat of terrorism by a number of radical groups from the Middle East. That strike lead directly to the installation of security checkpoints in airports all over the world. From 5:00 p.m. on Saturday until 9:00 a.m. on Monday, more than 50,000 commercial airline pilots refused to fly. My flight from Asmara, Ethiopia, landed in Athens, Greece, after noon on Saturday, where I got stuck for two days. Tough duty! The Aegean Sea is breathtakingly beautiful, Athens is incredible, the food is unbelievable and the nights are alive with excitement.

Leaving the Army

Under military law, every general court-martial conviction results in an automatic review by the Court of Military Appeals. Lawyers assigned to the Defense Appellate Section and Government Appellate Section of the JAGC office in Washington, DC argue these cases on appeal. John Toland, my pledge brother at the Beta House at KU and my roommate for two years in law school, incredibly was assigned to represent the defendant in my murder case. He argued on appeal that the sentence should be reduced because the color photographs of the victim showing the 42 stab wounds were unnecessarily inflammatory. His argument was rejected.

More importantly to me, John informed me that a draft regulation would soon be implemented permitting JAGC officers to leave the service early if they were enrolled in a graduate program. I applied for admission to the Master of Laws programs at Texas, Michigan, Yale and Harvard. I was accepted by Harvard and given a full-tuition scholarship. I did not get accepted at Yale, Texas or Michigan.

I submitted my resignation application and walked it through channels in Europe, but it was denied. I learned that Major General Prue, the two star Judge Advocate General of the Army, who had been the Judge Advocate General for US Army Europe before his promotion, would be making a tour of the JAGC offices in Germany. With the permission of COL Davis, I telephoned Washington from Germany, requesting that I have five minutes of General Prue's time during his scheduled visit to TASCOM headquarters. Three weeks later, General Prue arrived. He spent more than an hour encouraging the seventeen lawyers in the JAGC office at TASCOM headquarters to remain in the service and to continue their career in the military.

The early out regulation had not yet been published. After this meeting, he instructed everyone to leave except me. He addressed me directly: "What in the hell are you doing applying for graduate law school in view of your commitment to the Army?" I told him that

I had learned about the draft early out program. I had made application to LL.M programs at Harvard, Yale, Texas and Michigan. I also told him that I had been accepted at Harvard, that Harvard had awarded me a full-tuition scholarship and that both my acceptance and the scholarship were contingent upon me entering the program in September 1972.

In making application to resign my Army commission, I literally walked my application through channels, which required me to gain the approval of COL Davis, my direct boss, the headquarters Commandant, the Chief of Staff and the Commanding General at TASCOM, as well as the Judge Advocate General, US Army Europe and the Commanding General, US Army Europe, both in Heidelberg. I literally walked my application through channels, requesting an opportunity to meet each commander and presenting to that commander an order already drafted for his signature, approving the request. Some of my other friends had made application to resign from the service, and their applications had taken as long as four or five months to clear US Army Europe. My application cleared US Army Europe with approvals at every level of the command in twelve hours.

Upon my return from Ethiopia, after trying the "lying son of a bitch" case, I received orders accepting my resignation request and ordering me to exit the service in three days. I was required to get a complete physical exam, make arrangements for the shipment of our household goods from Germany to the US, drive my car to Bremerhaven for shipment to the United States and say goodbye. Once again, angels surrounded me, guiding me through the resignation process and permitting me to enroll at Harvard Law School in Cambridge, MA. I will always be grateful for the opportunity to serve in the Army and to have been assigned to serve under COL York at Fort Lewis and COL Davis in Germany.

Harvard
1972-1973

Claudia and I left Germany and returned to the US in early August 1972. After visiting Tulsa and Pratt, we journeyed to Cambridge one week before classes started at Harvard. That was not much time to find housing, enroll and get settled. We were shocked at the poor housing quality and high prices. We rented the second floor of a three story house owned by an odd old couple in Belmont, Massachusetts, five miles from campus.

I took classes in Estate Planning from Professor Casner, Federal Courts and the Federal System from Professor Bator, Labor Law from Archibald Cox, and Legal Process from Dean Sacks, among others. It was awesome to be in class with students who worked so hard and were so smart and from teachers who were the absolute tops in their fields. I selected a topic in labor law involving the employer's duty to bargain with the union when a company proposed the sale of one of its plants as my LLM thesis topic. My advisor was Archibald Cox, who was a notoriously low grader but who gave me the only A+ in my entire student career. Claudia typed the paper three times on a manual typewriter. My paper was published in the Minnesota Law Review without any changes or editorial comments or revisions. My paper has been cited by the US Supreme Court.

While at Harvard, the 1972 Olympics were being held in Munich. We watched in horror as terrorists killed many members of the Israeli Olympic team. Only weeks earlier, Claudia and I had walked the Olympic stadium field in Munich, before the innocence of the Olympic spirit was destroyed forever.

I accepted a $500 research project for Professor Sutherland's extraordinary book on the legal process in America. He footnoted reference to the young Army captain who first wore a robe as a trial judge in special court-martial cases, though he did not mention my name.

While I was attending the Harvard LL.M program, Royena, Claudia's mom, came to Boston for a visit. We walked the Freedom Trail, ate lobster at Anthony's and saw Sergio Ozwa conduct the Boston Pops. How awesome!82I interviewed for a permanent job with law firms in Minneapolis, Tulsa and Dallas. After considering my alternatives, I accepted a position with Jackson, Walker, Winstead, Cantwell & Miller in Dallas. Jackson Walker paid for trips for Claudia and me to fly to Dallas, including a spring break trip to search for housing. We were wined and dined at fancy restaurants and exclusive country clubs. Lawyers at Jackson Walker made me feel important, welcomed and needed. I negotiated a compensation package with an annual salary of $15,500 ($500 more than offered to the four other law students coming out of school), with an agreement that I would report for work on June 1, 1973, but that I would be paid but not be required to work during the three week bar review course prior to taking the Texas Bar in July 1973. I believed that I needed time off to study for the bar, since it had been five years since I had studied any of the materials likely to be on the test.

One week before leaving Harvard, Archibald Cox was appointed Independent Counsel in the Watergate investigation. I thought that destiny had tapped me on the shoulder. I called Mr. Cox's office and home several times, intending to volunteer to help him, even though I had accepted a job with Jackson Walker in Dallas. Fortunately for me, the line was always busy. Once again, angels guided me and protected me from myself and from being involved in the Watergate prosecution.

Jackson Walker
1973-1976

Claudia and I drove from Boston to Dallas in late May. We were anxious to start working in Dallas, so I skipped Harvard graduation. I wish I had stayed for graduation, but we needed to start making some money. We actually drove through a small tornado while driving through rural Alabama. Debris flew all over. Thankfully, the tornado had just passed and my angels were on duty during this trip.

We moved into our new home in far North Dallas on May 30, 1973. We purchased our first mattress and slept on the floor that first night, waiting for our household goods shipments coming from Boston, Seattle and Baltimore from our time in the Army. All of these shipments were scheduled to arrive simultaneously the next day, which miraculously they did.

On Monday, I was once again welcomed into the offices of Jackson Walker. I was assigned to the Corporate Section, consisting of ten lawyers headed by Richard Whitesell, the person with whom I negotiated my employment and compensation package. A lunch was scheduled for the entire corporate group at a family style barbeque joint later that day. Family style barbeque dining was more my style than the fancy restaurants and the country club meals we had received in the past. That first lunch was a disaster.

Dick Whitesell dominated the conversation at lunch. He emphasized the importance of being a team player, making numerous sarcastic references to younger lawyers from other states and schools outside of Texas, specifically referring to Harvard. He did not mention me specifically by name, but everyone at the table knew who he was talking about, especially me. The comments were threatening and unpleasant and implied that I was somehow not a team player and that I had better become one soon. I was mystified and hurt by the comments, particularly since I had no idea what gave rise to such comments. I learned that one of the other four new lawyers wanted the same deal I had negotiated. The implication was that nobody with the talent of Jackson Walker's new hires should have any concerns about passing the bar, without special study arrangements.

I was furious. After lunch, I immediately went into Dick Whitesell's office, closed the door and expressed my shock, anger and hurt. I could not believe that he would imply that I was not a team player to the other lawyers, because I negotiated and he personally agreed to arrangements that we both felt were appropriate. The implication was that I was somehow undermining the law firm by reaching an agreement which he personally approved. That agreement was unusual at the time. It had been five years since I had taken the Kansas bar, and I had been trying criminal cases and going to school outside of Texas during those five years. The arrangement to allow me time to study for the bar with pay is a customary benefit extended to new hires today. It clearly was an appropriate provision for me to ask for, and it certainly did not undermine the firm or in any way make me not a team player.

I told Mr. Whitesell that if he did not want me to be in the firm or if he wanted to negotiate a change in the agreement which he made with me, the proper thing for him to do would be for him to come to me outside the presence of other lawyers and discuss his concerns. I told Mr. Whitesell that if he did not want me in the firm, I would leave, because I had two other offers from prestigious law firms in Dallas. I also warned him that he was never ever to treat anyone the way he treated me. He reconfirmed again that I would come to work during the bar review process, and my job during that time was to study for the bar. This first lunch destroyed any opportunity for me to succeed at Jackson Walker. I stayed at Jackson Walker for three years before leaving on December 31, 1976, to join another Dallas firm.

Boundary Dispute

On May 30, 1973, Claudia and I moved into our first home at 15735 Regal Hill Circle in North Dallas. We were so excited to have a new house, but our excitement was diminished by a boundary dispute between me and my next-door neighbor that led to a significant crisis in our 120 home residential development. There were eight half-circles with houses built both on the inside and outside of the circles. There was an open area in the middle, containing tennis courts, a big swimming pool and other recreational and park facilities. My next-door neighbor was president of the homeowners' association.

The very first time I mowed my lawn, I mowed the lawn down the property line on the south side of my house. There were no windows on that side of my house, and my neighbor staked his large Great Dane against my house. When I began to mow, my neighbor came running out to stop me, saying that I was mowing part of his property. I said that I did not believe the land belonged to him. I consulted my certified survey and my deed and pointed out to him that I was simply mowing the grass on my property. He claimed to have a "recreational easement" that covered all the way to the south side of my house. There was no recorded easement on my deed or survey. I was very concerned about his dog biting someone on my property and being held responsible. I asked him to remove his dog.

I decided to build a fence down the property line like other houses in the addition. The homeowners' association rules required approval of the construction of a fence. My neighbor was president of the homeowners' association and head of the architectural control committee. He told me that no privacy fence would be approved for my property. He also told me that if I sought to build one, he would use legal action to stop me. That was not nice.

The next day the senior partner of a large major Dallas law firm's real estate section called me to discuss the issue. He explained that the homes in this development had been built on a "zero lot line" concept and that was why there were no windows on the south side of my house. The problem was that the zero lot line violated the Dallas building code 10% setback requirement on each side and in the back of each home.

I agreed to grant my neighbor an easement, provided the homeowners' association grant me an easement on common property to my east and north. Sixty-six homes out of the 120 homes had fences, swimming pools, landscaping and permanent structures built across property lines, and no recorded easements had to be granted to any of those property owners. The neighbors were furious, because they thought an upstart lawyer from Harvard caused this problem, when in fact, they should have been pleased, since I was able to force a resolution of serious title survey problems that each one of those homeowners would have faced when selling their home.

While I was entirely and legally correct, this property dispute had an adverse effect upon how we were treated by our neighbors. Within three years, we moved to a new house at 16001 Windy Meadow, approximately half mile west of our first home.

Associated Milk Producers

1973 was a time of great turmoil politically. The Watergate investigation was in full bloom, with my LL.M thesis advisor, Archibald Cox, leading the Independent Counsel's investigation of President Nixon's role in the Watergate break in. Within a month after arriving at Jackson Walker, I was ask to go with Mr. Hartman, a senior Jackson Walker litigator, to assist in representing Associated Milk

Producers, Inc. ("AMPI") in connection with subpoenas which had been served on that national milk lobbying organization arising out of the Watergate investigation. It was alleged that the $50,000 cash found in the possession of the burglars was paid by John Connolly with funds provided by AMPI.

AMPI was represented generally by Jenner & Block, a prestigious politically astute law firm in Chicago. Jenner & Block engaged Jackson Walker as Texas counsel for the sole purpose of determining the scope of AMPI's attorney-client privilege under Texas law. The Watergate subpoenas were incredibly broad, seeking virtually all the records of AMPI in connection with any contact with present or former members of Congress, especially all contacts with their lawyers and lobbyists. AMPI is one of the largest and one of the most effective lobbying organizations in the country. Its members include virtually every dairy farmer in the country, and its war chest was huge.

It was ironic for me to be involved in this matter, since only six weeks earlier, five days before completing final exams at Harvard, Archibald Cox had been selected as the Independent Counsel to lead the investigations into the Watergate allegations. I could have been on the other side of the subpoena issue for AMPI.

Upon arriving at AMPI headquarters in San Antonio, I was directed to a large warehouse with rows and rows and rows of boxes containing nothing but invoices from law firms for "professional services rendered and expenses incurred." My job was to identify all papers that involved a valid claim of attorney-client privilege. The task was enormous. The time to respond was short. Almost every paper in AMPI's files related to election campaigns and specific legislative proposals in Congress and was therefore covered by the subpoena. The results of the effort were virtually preordained, since no one really believed that AMPI would not disclose documents to the Watergate investigators on attorney-client privilege grounds, no matter how valid the position was.

Two weeks later a group of eleven FBI agents and three investigators from the Independent Counsel's office descended upon San Antonio with the specific objective of finding any incriminating papers against either President Richard Nixon or Navy Secretary John Connolly. John Connolly had twice been elected Governor of Texas as a Democrat, and he was in the car when President Kennedy was assassinated, but he had resigned from the Democratic Party and become a Republican. He was the most likely Republican nominee for President to succeed Richard Nixon. There were allegations, however, that John Connolly had personally delivered the cash paid to the conspirators who broke into the Democratic National Campaign offices in the Watergate complex and that the money came from AMPI. He was tried but acquitted of those criminal charges, but the trial destroyed John Connolly's future political and professional aspirations.

The AMPI records I reviewed consisted of invoices from law firms all over the country, most of which were for unspecified "legal services rendered and expenses incurred," and huge fees were sought. It was later alleged that many law firms illegally funneled political campaign contributions to candidates for federal office by inflating invoices for services rendered and passing excessive payments on to the respective campaigns. The AMPI records contained law firm invoices on both sides of almost every contest in virtually every House and Senate race in the country, including virtually every preliminary and run off race. AMPI supported both Democratic and Republican candidates, so that it would have a place at the table no matter who won. Numerous election campaign reprimands, fines and other punishments were later inflicted upon many members of the House and Senate because of the receipt of illegal campaign donations from law firms.

My First Closing

During my first year at Jackson Walker, one relatively simple matter was assigned to me. The mayor of Dallas and his wife were wealthy by reason of his ownership of a major commercial construction firm. The mayor and his wife each had complicated trusts in which various parcels of land, stocks, bonds and other assets had been contributed. The mayor and his wife desired to revise and update the language in the trust documents and to exchange and reposition various items of personal property. My job was to review the trust documents, make appropriate changes, change the schedules of assets in each trust to reflect which assets were to be owned by what trust, and prepare the final papers for closing.

My first business closing was to occur on a Monday. Because the transaction involved the mayor and his wife and properties managed by three different large banks, the presidents of each bank and their counsel came to the closing. On the Thursday before closing, the documents were in final form and perfectly correct. Nevertheless, I continued to read and review them on Friday to ensure that there were absolutely perfect. I rarely went to the office on Saturday, but because this was my first closing, I wanted to review the documents one more time just to make sure that everything was correct.

Laura, my daughter, was three months old at the time. I decided to take her to the office while I reviewed the documents. My desk was a very large old oak partner's desk with a large overhang all the way around the desk. I put Laura on the desk while I read the trust documents. Unfortunately, Laura wet her pants all over the trust and closing documents. The phrase "piss on it" comes to mind when I think of this disaster. I had to arrange to have a secretary come to the office on Sunday to print out a fresh set of the papers. I made no changes in the documents on Saturday or Sunday, since they were just as correct then as they had been on the previous Thursday.

At this time the word processing equipment used IBM magnetic cards, one card for each page. The trust documents consisted of a stack of IBM cards with all the personal pronouns in the mayor's document being masculine in gender and all of the personal pronouns in the mayor's wife's trust instrument being feminine. The secretary accidentally dropped the cards and put the back half of the wife's trust with the front half of the mayor's trust. The result was that the gender of the pronouns changed halfway through the documents. Except for that, the documents were letter perfect. I did not catch the error, and the secretary did not tell me what had happened.

One of the bank lawyers caught the error in the middle of the closing. We had to redo the documents while everyone waited. I was terribly embarrassed. Since that time, I have always been extremely cautious when approaching a closing. I try never to set a closing on a Friday afternoon or a Monday morning. I do not allow anyone to put liquids on the closing table where the closing documents are waiting to be signed and assembled. I also learned that once the papers are perfect, do not fix or fool around with them again. Any change will almost surely be disruptive.

Jackson Hole

Menial tasks always flow downhill to the youngest guy in a law office. That was the case when Jackson Walker represented Mercantile of Texas in the formation of one of the top twenty bank holding companies in the country. Federally chartered banking organizations are permitted to engage only in banking activities, but not in related services. In the early 1970s there were a great number of bank holding companies formed to provide accounting, record keeping, stock transfer, trust department and other services not directly involved with commercial banking per se.

Mercantile of Texas was organized as a Texas corporation. Approval by the US Comptroller of the Currency and other federal regulatory agencies was required to consummate the merger of the existing acquisition target into the new bank holding company. The initial organizational meeting of the board of directors of Mercantile of Texas took place by written consent, except that not all directors had signed the consent as required by Texas law.

Several months after Mercantile of Texas was organized, Jackson Walker was engaged to complete the regulatory approval process. I was one of the associates assigned to conduct due diligence of related documents to ensure the transaction was accurately and legally conducted. Approvals from the Comptroller of the Currency were scheduled to become effective on a Monday. On the prior Thursday afternoon, we discovered that some of the directors had not signed the unanimous consent of the first organizational meeting. One of the persons who did not sign the written consent had left Dallas earlier that day with his wife and another couple on a camping trip to Yellowstone National Park. After considerable effort, we located that director and made arrangements for him to sign the written consent the following day, before leaving for parts unknown. I was assigned the task of getting his signature on the written consent.

I flew out of Dallas at 5:00 a.m. Friday morning with a connecting flight through Denver. Fifteen minutes after the Denver flight left for Jackson Hole, the right engine of the 727 shut down. The pilot diverted to Cheyenne. I was to meet the director at his hotel in Jackson Hole before noon on Friday. He made it quite clear that if I was not there by noon, he would be in Yellowstone National Park in an unknown location for two weeks. After more than two hours on the ground in Cheyenne, my diverted fight was not going to arrive in Jackson Hole before noon.

I used my personal MasterCard to charter a private airplane for the flight from Cheyenne to Jackson Hole. The weather was clear, but the flight was incredibly turbulent. I threw up all over the front seat of the private aircraft. Upon landing in Jackson Hole, I discovered that the airport was nine miles from the town of Jackson Hole, and there were no cabs, vans, delivery services or other means of transportation from the airport to downtown Jackson Hole. I called the director at his hotel, and he agreed to drive by the airport on his way into Yellowstone. I always carried extra pens in my briefcase, but that day, not a single one of them worked. As a result, the director used his wife's mascara pen to sign the written consent on the hood of their Suburban with the Grand Tetons in the background. My task was accomplished. All I had to do was get back to Dallas.

When I tried to board the next flight out of Jackson Hole, I was told that if "you get on that plane, that plane will not clear those mountains." About that time, the replacement plane that was flown from Dallas arrived in Jackson Hole, and I returned to Denver on that flight. We arrived in Denver at one end of Stapleton, but my connecting flight to Dallas was at the other end of Stapleton. I ran the distance but the stewardess closed the door to the airplane in front of me, not allowing me to board that flight. I had no money and I had tapped out my credit renting the plane to take me to Jackson Hole, so I spent the night in the Stapleton airport and took the first flight out to Dallas the next morning. My mission was accomplished by almost absurd efforts to get one signature on a document which should have been signed months earlier. My angels were there to help me do what was required, even when extraordinary events occur.

Sol Ravinski

One of the popular radio programs in the 1940s was entitled the "Whiz Kids." Four incredibly bright prodigies around twelve years old would answer questions from listeners who called during the program about seemingly minute details on an infinite variety of subjects. Sol Ravinski was one of the first Whiz Kids. In his later life, he married one of the daughters of a founder of Zale Corporation, the jewelry giant headquartered in Dallas.

Mr. Ravinski was also allegedly a thief. His job at the Zale Corporation was vice president and chief financial officer of Zale. In that capacity he was responsible for filing federal income tax returns. Zale had approximately 1,800 stores, each of which was separately incorporated to take advantage of a federal income tax break. As CFO. Mr. Ravinski filed separate tax returns for each store and allegedly intentionally overstated the income. Later, he filed a request for a refund. When the refund checks were received, he allegedly deposited them in his own personal bank account at the same bank where Zale banked. A first year internal auditor blew the whistle on this scheme. Mr. Ravinski was charged with stealing over a $1.6 million in federal income tax refunds. His employment was terminated and state criminal charges were filed against him.

Mr. Ravinski asserted that the Board of Directors had authorized him to keep the tax refunds to keep him silent about bribes paid to diamond dealers in Tel Aviv, Belgium, Rotterdam and other diamond trading centers. The IRS initiated its first major investigation under the newly adopted Foreign Corrupt Practices Act against Zale, and the SEC stopped trading in Zale stock and commenced a major investigation.

In the first state court embezzlement prosecution of Mr. Ravinski, the jury hung. He was tried again and acquitted. The SEC and IRS investigations found no illegal payments made by Zale to diamond dealers or others. In settling the SEC investigation with a consent decree, Zale was required to hire new counsel and new accountants and replace some of its outside directors with new outside directors. Sam Winstead, the senior tax partner at Jackson Walker, was a Zale director. Jackson Walker lost a major account as a result of the consent decree. In my view, it is not wise for lawyers in a firm to serve on the Board of Directors of its clients.

Curlee Clothing Proxy Fight

Curlee Clothing Company, headquartered in St. Louis, was a major manufacturer of distinguished men's suits for more than 75 years when the leisure suit craze hit in the early 1970s. Curlee had only 350 shareholders, so it was not a 1934 Act reporting company and not required to file periodic reports with the SEC or comply with SEC's proxy rules. Most of the shareholders were employees who bought their shares when Mr. Curlee's estate needed money to pay estate taxes.

In the early 1970s, Curlee suffered significant operating losses, largely due to the leisure suit craze and perhaps because of poor management. Phillip Laughlin, son of a former president, led a group seeking to replace the president and other senior managers and half of the Board. To ensure secrecy, the insurgent group engaged Jackson Walker in Dallas to assist in the proxy fight that occurred. I was assigned to represent the insurgent group in drafting proxy materials.

Because the insurgent group included some senior officers, we were able to obtain the company's proposed shareholder communications, financial information and shareholder's list without a fight. We made numerous mailings, some of which were sent overnight to arrive before the company's own shareholder materials arrived. We reduced the company's materials in size, and highlighted specific negative financial data. We used blue proxy cards for the insurgent's Board nominees, replacing six inside Board members with nominees from the insurgent group. At one point in time, we had received proxy's representing more than 75% of the outstanding shares.

Around noon on Thursday before the scheduled annual shareholders' meeting on the following Tuesday, I received a call from counsel to the company, indicating that a motion for a temporary restraining order had been filed in Clayton County District Court and a hearing had been scheduled at 3:30 p.m. that same day. I immediately left my office in Dallas and flew to St. Louis, arriving at the courthouse in Clayton at 3:45 p.m. The trial judge invited counsel into his chambers. He addressed me as Mr. Slicker from Texas and Bob, John and Larry from St. Louis. Company counsel, Bryan Cave, was the largest law firm in Missouri. A group of fifteen lawyers, led by the recently retired Chief Judge for the Court of Appeals in St. Louis, Bob Brady, represented Curlee.

A motion for a temporary restraining order, seeking to enjoin the voting of insurgent proxies and alleging fraud and material misrepresentations in the insurgent group's proxy material, was discussed at length by St. Louis counsel. Mr. Brady indicated irreparable injury would incur if the court did not enjoin the voting of those proxies. The trial judge turned to me for a response. I stated that my witnesses on these issues were in the courtroom and that we were ready to proceed with a hearing on the motion, denying all the allegations and asserting that the only reason for the company's motion was to illicitly and wrongfully keep current management in their high paying non-producing corporate jobs. By this time it was almost 5:00 p.m. The trial judge was impressed, but he declined to hold a hearing that evening. Instead, he noticed a hearing for 9:00 a.m. the following morning.

At 8:45 a.m. on Friday, the trial judge received a mandamus from the St. Louis Court of Appeals, enjoining the trial judge from holding a hearing on Curlee's temporary restraining order motion. He and I were mystified. The company proposed an aggressive discovery schedule, which would cover the next four to six weeks, long past the holding of the annual meeting. The allegations were frivolous and intended solely to impede the insurgents from voting proxies which had legitimately been sought and obtained. A hearing was scheduled at 1:30 p.m. in the Court of Appeals for St. Louis before a three judge panel to consider the mandamus motion filed by the company seeking to prevent the trial judge from holding the TRO hearing which the company had sought. The three judges on the panel served under the direct supervision of Bob Brady only weeks before, but he was now lead counsel for the company. It was extraordinary and only because of Judge Brady's influence that a three judge panel could be convened on one day's notice. After two hours of arguments, the Court of Appeals denied Bob Brady's mandamus motion and returned the matter to the District Court for trial. By this time it was approximately 3:30 p.m. on Friday before the scheduled annual shareholders' meeting the following Tuesday.

I had arranged local St. Louis counsel to assist me in litigating these issues. We concluded that we needed counsel in Jefferson City where the state Supreme Court was located, because we anticipated Judge Brady pulling additional personal strings to keep our client from voting proxies lawfully obtained. Consequently, we flew in a chartered plane almost 150 miles from St. Louis to Jefferson City and met into the night with an elder statesman of the state bar who was also a close personal friend and golf companion of the Chief Justice of the Supreme Court of Missouri. We brought with us all the related papers, so that he would be fully informed of the events surrounding these extraordinary proceedings. To our surprise, no extraordinary relief was filed over the weekend.

On Monday morning at 9:00 a.m., the day prior to the scheduled annual shareholders' meeting, the company's TRO motion was heard. At 4:30 p.m. on Monday, the trial court denied the company's motion, specifically found there was no showing of fraud or misrepresentation and specifically held that the insurgents' proxies were valid and must be counted.

Judge Brady took the extraordinary step of bypassing the St. Louis Court of Appeals and filed a mandamus action before the Missouri Supreme Court in front of his longtime friend, the Chief Justice. From 8:30 p.m. Monday evening until 1:30 a.m. Tuesday morning, the company and its entourage of lawyers and me and my local counsel appeared in the chambers in the Chief Justice of the Supreme Court of the State of Missouri, considering the extraordinary remedies sought by the company. At the conclusion of the hearing, the Chief Justice turned to Mr. Brady and said, "Bob, I see no factual basis for the relief requested." He denied the company's extraordinary relief.

The following morning at 10:00 a.m., in an auditorium filled with more than 300 persons, Curlee Clothing Company's annual shareholders' meeting was called to order. Votes were cast, an election committee was appointed, the company's accounting firm was selected to tabulate the votes and the meeting was adjourned until counting had been completed. Over the next twelve hours, the parties argued over every single proxy from every single shareholder, many of whom had sent in proxies for both sides, with the latest ballot being the one required to be counted. My clients won by approximately 1,400 votes out of approximately 500,000 shares voting. The company requested that a recount be conducted to ensure accuracy. The chairman of the election committee agreed and set the recount for the following morning at 8:00 a.m.

The recount confirmed the insurgent group's victory, but before the results were announced, the chairman of the company, who was about to lose his high paying corporate job, announced the reopening of the election, indicating that three shareholders had changed their votes. Three shareholders represented a loss of approximately 1,500 votes for the insurgents and a gain of an equal amount for the company. A fist fight erupted when Phillip Laughlin, my client, tried to take over the microphone from the company's chairman. A lady in the rear of the room picked up a twenty-gallon coffee pot filled with hot coffee, and threw it at one of my local lawyers. I was incensed and spoke out vehemently, delaying the recount and instructing my local counsel to file suit locally to seek a court order to maintain the status quo and to enjoin the announcement of this fraudulent recount. This litigation was settled after weeks of vicious fighting with five old board members remaining on the board, five new insurgent nominees added to the board, and one neutral board member being selected by both groups. The results were a victory snatched fraudulently from the jaws of defeat by management of the company.

It was later discovered that one of the three shareholders who changed her vote because the company paid her $15 a share, when the stock was valued pre-proxy fight at less than $4 a share. Another shareholder changed her vote when her husband was threatened with the loss of all work from the company. He was its local labor lawyer; and the company's labor work represented most of this practice. A third shareholder changed his vote when he was promised a raise and a long-term employment agreement with a better title and more benefits. It is hard not to blame the three shareholders involved. It is easy to blame Judge Brady, his firm and the unscrupulous misconduct of the company and its lawyers in defeating the will of the owners of the company in favor of personal financial arrangements of incompetent management. Welcome to the real world!

Leaving Jackson Walker

My unhappiness at Jackson Walker began with the first day at work and continued daily with lousy assignments and no favorable feedback through 1976. I felt compelled to begin interviewing at other law firms. I received offers from a large Corpus Christi firm and a general counsel position for a very wealthy Texan, who owned significant oil and gas interests in the United States and enormous land holdings in Australia. Neither position seemed right for me.

In early November 1976, I was contacted by an oil and gas company headquartered in Oklahoma City whose stock was traded on the New York Stock Exchange. After an initial interview, I was invited back for a second interview and was extended an employment offer as Vice President and General Counsel on Wednesday, the day before Thanksgiving. During our drive back to Dallas, I told Claudia that I intended to accept the offer at 10:00 a.m. on Monday morning, but I was still negotiating for a company car and a country club membership similar to the benefits being paid to the other senior officers of this company.

The offer was for a $70,000 annual salary, twice my current compensation, plus annual bonuses and significant stock options. The company's books were audited by Arthur Anderson of Houston, a highly respected national accounting firm. The firm was engaged in numerous transactions using both cash and stock in an effort to acquire operating properties and oil and gas equipment. The work would be exciting, significant and interesting.

At 9:45 a.m. on Monday morning, fifteen minutes before I planned to accept the offer, I received a telephone call from a person I have never met, whose name I never knew. He said that he knew that I was interviewing in Oklahoma City, that he had inquired about my background and experience and that he had concluded that I was not right for the position and should not accept it. I was shocked. I sought to meet the caller, but he refused to talk further. I asked whom he had talked with in Oklahoma City, but he declined to say. All he said was that his conscience was clear, because he had called to urge me to decline the offer. Finally, this caller said that I should contact the former general counsel, who had accepted a position with National Gypsum Company, a major New York Stock Exchange company whose headquarters had recently moved from Buffalo, New York, to Dallas.

I called the former general counsel, identified myself and asked if I could take him to lunch. He said that he was too busy. I persisted and he finally relented. During that two hour conversation, this former general counsel told me things about the company which may have violated his attorney-client privilege but which also convinced me that I should not accept the position. Upon returning from lunch, I called Oklahoma City and declined the offer. The company offered more money to persuade me to change my mind, which I also declined. On that day, God's angels worked overtime to protect me from a very bad situation which looked too good to be true. It was!

During my three years at Jackson Walker, Laura was born on April 5, 1976. This was a joyous and unbelievably happy occasion. She weighed only five pounds, ten ounces. She was so small and so gentle, and she did not even open her eyes for several weeks, but she transformed my life. I had not gone to the expectant father's classes, and I did not even know where the emergency room at the hospital was. Somehow, we found our way there the night she was born. I waited in the expectant father's room. The only other person there was an expectant grandfather, who was 38 and whose second daughter was having her second child. I was 31, and Laura was our first. Six weeks later my father died. He got to see and hold Laura before his lungs gave out. My father was 63 when he died of complications from emphysema and two previous heart attacks and years of smoking three packs a day.

Kipp was born two years later on September 5, 1976. This time at least I knew where the hospital was. Compared to Laura, Kipp was almost full grown at birth. He weighed nine pounds, ten ounces. What a blessing and what a joy both Laura and Kipp have been to me throughout my life. Life would be hollow and empty without having had the privilege of being their dad. God's angels have worked overtime helping me be the best dad I could be for them. They have blessed me beyond belief by who they are. What a joy they have been for me and Claudia!

Worsham Forsythe & Sampels
1977-1980

I left Jackson Walker on December 31, 1976, after accepting a position with Worsham Forsythe & Sampels, a twelve lawyer firm in downtown Dallas. I had expressed a desire to continue to work on securities offerings, but I also wanted to work in litigation. At Worsham Forsythe, I was both a litigator and a securities lawyer, and it just about drove me crazy. Sometimes it is not good to have your wish come true!

The Electric Range War

I was hired primarily to assist Merlin Sampels in representing Texas Utilities Company (TU) in what would become a massive struggle for the electric utility industry in Texas to remain free from federal regulation. One of the principal causes of the Great Depression was the monopolistic positions held by a very small number of electric utility holding companies. These companies not only generated and supplied electricity, but they also supplied natural gas and even manufactured and distributed ice to their customers, among other services.

The Public Utility Holding Company Act of 1935 was the legislative response to ensure that the electric utility industry would no longer come under such massive monopolistic power. The preamble to that Act states that it is against federal public policy for there to be an interstate electric utility holding company. As a result, in the late

1930s and early 1940s, while the world braced for world war, the six or seven massive interstate electric utility holding companies were forced to divest subsidiaries providing electricity across state lines. What developed were three interconnected electric utility grids, one for the eastern portion of the United States, another for the western portion of the United States and the third for Texas.

TU owned three operating subsidiaries which supplied electric service to customers in northeastern Texas comprising approximately one-third of the entire state. TU consisted of Dallas Power & Light Company (DPL), which served the city of Dallas; Texas Power & Light Company (TPL), which served most of northeastern Texas, and Texas Electric Service Company (TESCO), which served Fort Worth and surrounding areas. All of these companies operated solely intrastate in Texas.

The 1973 Arab oil embargo caused a national policy shift from gas-fired to coal-fired electric generation. Coal was not sufficiently plentiful in Texas, so coal had to be purchased and transported from Montana to Texas. Mining coal is very expensive, but the railroad charges to transport the coal to south Texas are extraordinarily expensive, monopolistic.

In response to the Arab oil embargo, the US electric utility industry began designing and constructing nuclear power plants. Because nuclear energy had been developed by the federal government, federal policy required that any nuclear power plant obtain a construction license before the plant could commence construction, and an operating license must be obtained before the plant could commence operations. It was thought that nuclear energy would be significantly cheaper than coal or natural gas fired energy plants, so nuclear power plants could have a massive adverse impact upon competition, especially with local municipal electric systems and rural electric cooperatives. An antitrust review was a mandatory requirement in the construction and operating permit licensing process.

Companies that generate electricity interconnect with neighboring electric systems to prevent outages in the event of storms, tornadoes or other disasters. TU was a fully interconnected electric utility holding company, but each of its contracts with neighboring systems prohibited them sending or receiving power from out-of-state sources. All TU companies operated solely in Texas. TU built its generation, transmission and distribution system on the intrastate model, and TU spent hundreds of millions of dollars developing an electric transmission network which did not serve electric loads outside of Texas, except in times of war or electrical emergency. Federal Power Commission (FPC) orders exempted TU from the Public Utility Holding Company Act during times of electric emergency, for example, during World War II.

Comanche Park was a nuclear powered station south of Fort Worth owned by TU. Extensive hearings at the FPC and the Atomic Energy Commission resulted in granting a license for the construction of Comanche Peak. An extensive antitrust review during the construction phase centered on TU's policy prohibiting others connected to TU from sending or receiving electric power outside of Texas. Likewise, Houston Lighting & Power (HLP), with the city of Austin, the city of San Antonio and various rural electric utility systems, proposed to construct a nuclear powered station called the South Texas Project (STP). All of their interconnection agreements prohibited other systems from receiving or sending power in interstate commerce.

Central & Southwest Corporation (CSW) is an electric utility holding company operating through four electric utility subsidiaries: Public Service Company of Oklahoma (PSO) headquartered in Tulsa; Southwest Electric Power (SWEP) headquartered in Shreveport, LA; West Texas Utilities (WTU) headquartered in Lubbock, TX; and Central Power & Light (CPL) headquartered in Corpus Christi. TX. CSW operated WTU and CLP with other Texas companies solely in Texas. All their interconnection contracts prohibited any other system from sending or receiving electric power outside of Texas. CPL and WTU were interconnected with HLP and TU. CSW operated PSO and SWEP in interstate commerce and were not connected to the Texas systems.

In 1972, the city of Frederick, Oklahoma, filed a massive petition with the Securities and Exchange Commission (SEC), asserting that CSW was in fact an unlawful interstate electric utility holding company operating in violation of the Public Utility Holding Company Act. CSW, PSO and SWEP operated in interstate commerce and were subject to federal rate regulation, but CPL and WTU, which operated solely in Texas, were not. The city of Frederick's application sought to reduce the wholesale electric rates to cities like Frederick and threatened the very existence of CSW.

A hearing before the SEC on CWS' response was scheduled for May 12, 1976. CSW took preemptive action. At five minutes before the US District Court Clerk's office in Dallas closed on May 3, 1976, CSW filed an antitrust case against HLP and TU, alleging that their contracts, which prohibited interstate sale or receipt of electric power, violated the Sherman Antitrust Act. That night CSW sent a power crew from PSO in Tulsa to re-wire a WTU substation in Texas to permit electric power to flow from Texas into Oklahoma. The following morning when the FPC opened at 8:30 a.m. in Washington, an application was filed by CSW with the FPC, asserting that all of the electric utility companies in Texas were subject to federal jurisdiction by reason of power flowing into Oklahoma through the re-wired power station in west Texas. When TU and HLP learned of these actions, they disconnected from all other systems, creating an electrical emergency. This action spawned more than twenty different cases before numerous federal courts and federal and state administrative agencies. I was hired to assist Merlin Sampels in representing TU in maintaining its status as an intrastate electric utility holding company, not subject to rate or other regulation by the federal government.

I came to Worsham Forsythe & Sampels in January 1977, just before the SEC hearing to establish discovery schedules in the city of Frederick's case. A massive ice storm hit north Texas Wednesday night, knocking out power lines and disrupting bus and other public transportation systems. I got up at 4 a.m. I walked a mile to get a bus ride downtown and waited three hours in six degree temperature for the bus. I simply had to get to the office. I was supposed to accompany Merlin to assist him in the SEC hearings. This was my first week of work at my new firm. I was determined to succeed there. I was the only one at the office when I arrived. Merlin came in at about 3 p.m. to catch our 5 p.m. flight from at DFW. We left the downtown office at approximately 4:10 p.m. and drove like a bat out of hell to DFW over ice-covered roads. We got to DFW just in time to be the last persons on the flight before it departed. This was to become a pattern which Merlin was to repeat frequently. Merlin believed that waiting at the airport was an absolute waste of time. He calculated his trips in an effort to try to be the last person on every flight. That attitude absolutely drove me crazy.

My job was primarily to work on the proceedings before the new Texas Utilities Commission, proceedings before the SEC, the antitrust case in the US District Court in Northern Texas, the operating license proceedings before the Nuclear Regulatory Commission (NRC) and other proceedings before the FPC.

One case involved where the Texas-Oklahoma border was physically located. An FPC proceeding was held to determine whether the Dennison Dam built on the Red River between Texas and Oklahoma just north of Sherman, TX, was physically located in Texas or in Oklahoma. When the Dennison Dam was initially constructed by TPL, a TU subsidiary, it was clearly constructed on the Texas side of the river. The boundary line between Texas and Oklahoma is the center of the Red River. Over time, the river changed its course and a question was raised as to whether the TPL power plant at the Dennison Dam was in fact in Texas or Oklahoma. If it was in

Oklahoma, all of the other proceedings would have been unnecessary, since TPL would have been operating in interstate commerce, and by reason of being interconnected with the other TU companies, the entire TU system and all other systems connected to it would have been subject to federally established rates.

The central question in the SEC case was whether the SEC had the power to regulate wholesale and retail rates charged by HLP and TU. If they operated in interstate commerce, TU and HLP were subject to federal regulation. If they operated solely in Texas, federal jurisdiction did not attach. The central question in the Texas Utilities Commission case involved the integrity and reliability of the electric utility system in Texas. The question in the US District Court case was whether the agreements prohibiting interstate transportation of electric power violated the Sherman antitrust act. The main question in the FPC case was whether an electric utility company could exit interstate commerce by operating solely in a single state and thereby avoid federal regulation of its electric rates.

The United States Supreme Court, in a case involving Connecticut Light & Power in 1943, determined that it was constitutionally permissible for an electric utility company to so structure its business as to not subject itself to federal rate regulation and federal control. The Court said that if the company was not serving customers in interstate commerce, then the federal government had no jurisdiction over its rates.

The FPC requested an opinion from its general counsel immediately after the CSW application was filed. The General Counsel was the son of Tiny Gooch, lead counsel for TESCO. He wrote a short memo, opining that the FPC had no jurisdiction over the Texas companies, citing the *Connecticut* case. CSW argued that since the application to assert jurisdiction was made while power was crossing state lines, FPC jurisdiction attached at that moment, even though the power crossed state lines involuntarily. No evidentiary hearing was held by the FPC. The FPC unanimously dismissed CSW's application, holding that TU and HLP were permitted to operate solely in intrastate commerce. No antitrust issues were raised in CSW's original filing. In effect, the FPC held that no one could "shanghai" another into federal jurisdiction, which was the central holding of the *Connecticut* case.

The FPC's dismissal of the CSW application was appealed to the District of Columbia Circuit Court of Appeals. In its brief, CSW raised antitrust issues, which were not discussed by the FPC. CSW persuaded the Circuit Court to remand for further proceedings to inquire into whether or not the antitrust issues were properly raised.

Because the *Connecticut* case was a square holding by the United States Supreme Court and the Court of Appeals decision remanding the case to the FPC flew squarely in the face that opinion, I urged Merlin to take a writ of certiorari to the United States Supreme Court. Three days before the writ had to be filed, Merlin consented. I spent the next three days and nights at the printers, writing the brief that we filed with the United States Supreme Court. This is the only brief I have submitted to the United States Supreme Court.

The Court rules are very specific about the size of type, the margins used, the color of the cover of the brief and the contents of all the appendices. The brief had to be set in hot type at a financial printer's office. The rules required that every statute cited and every case cited had to be copied in the appendix for easy reference. The Public Utility Holding Company Act was cited in our brief. In the preamble to that Act, there is reference to the "act" of Congress. The typesetters instead set "ass" of Congress. Fortunately, I caught that error on the final pass before the brief was filed with the Supreme Court. The Court declined to hear the case.

The antitrust case in the Northern District of Texas resulted in a nine-week bench trial. My part was to write the briefs and control the documents and exhibits. The brief I wrote was adopted almost verbatim by the District Court. The Fifth Circuit Court of Appeals affirmed that decision. TU and HLP won that battle, but the war continued.

The world ganged up against the Texas companies at the NRC. Thirty-one third parties intervened against TU and HLP in the NRC proceedings that would decide whether operating permits would issue for Comanche Peak and the South Texas Project. The longest estimate for the trial was four years, and the shortest estimate was eighteen months. I would have been required to move to Washington for the duration of the trial. This was a motivating factor, along with Merlin's unbelievably negative attitude and work demands, for me to leave Worsham Forsythe & Sampels. This case was settled several months after I left the firm.

Mostek

When Texas Instruments refused to pursue the development of the microchip semi-conductor business, four of its mid-level executives left to form Mostek. In less than ten years, Mostek grew from four employees to over 6,000, riding the wave of the development of the microchip and personal computers. I had the opportunity to lawyer four public securities offerings for Mostek during a period of only three years.

Early in its history, Mostek had borrowed from a venture capital firm. The short-term strategy for Mostek was to raise money in a public offering every time market conditions seemed favorable, thereby reducing the venture capitalist's interest from 52% in the company down to less than 20%. The venture capital firm had piggyback registration rights on any offering the company filed. The mechanics of exercising the piggyback rights required thirty days' notice from Mostek before filing a registered public offering.

I prepared registration statements to be filed as soon as the market seemed most favorable. Notice was given by Mostek that a filing would be made three to five days before Mostek was ready to file. Mostek never gave thirty days' notice as it was required to do. On one occasion, I left the printers in Dallas at 2:30 a.m. on the red eye flight for Washington DC with three separate filing packages, one where Mostek was selling authorized but unissued shares, another where the venture capital firm was selling all its shares and the third where both Mostek and the venture capital firm were selling half the shares offered. I was instructed to call Dallas upon my arrival at the SEC to see which package to file.

The last public offering I filed for Mostek was declared effective in twenty-three days and closed in thirty days after Mostek instructed us to file. In that offering, Mostek raised more than $20 million at $23 a share. Two months later, Mostek was acquired in a friendly tender offer for $63 a share.

I also drafted and reviewed proxy materials, annual reports, quarterly reports and interim reports for Mostek. On one occasion Mostek's chairman wrote a letter to the shareholders that contained a statement to the effect that the invention of the microchip was to the modern world what the invention of the Gutenberg printing press was to the medieval world. The printing press transformed an illiterate world into a world in which every person had access to books. The printing press gave birth to the age of enlightenment. In the late 1970s, I could not visualize such a dramatic impact by the microchip. My vision was limited, and I was wrong, when I strongly advised Mostek not to make such a statement.

Wales Trucking

I negotiated and wrote an asset purchase agreement in which Gifford Hill, Inc., a pre-stressed concrete manufacturer, acquired Wales Trucking Company. The transaction was interesting because at the time, Interstate Commerce Commission approval was required for the sale of a majority interest in a licensed interstate trucking company. The objective was to obtain the rights to transport product into Arizona, Nevada and California. A direct stock purchase acquisition would have invoked extensive opposition at the ICC, so

Gilford Hill took a two step approach. First, it acquired substantially all the trucks and trailers from Wales; and two years later, Gifford Hill acquired all the stock. Since the trucks and trailers were already owned by Gifford Hill and were being operated by Gifford Hill in those states, no protest was filed.

At 4:30 p.m. one Thursday afternoon, Merlin Sampels instructed me to prepare an asset purchase agreement for the acquisition of substantially all the assets of Wales for an 8:30 a.m. meeting the following morning with Gifford Hill management. This was typical of Merlin. I stayed up all night and drafted a relatively standard form asset purchase agreement and delivered it to Merlin at 7:45 a.m. the following morning. I will never forget Merlin taking a red pen and marking through all of the representations and warranties I included for our client. Sixteen full drafts later, four months of acrimonious negotiations and more than $60,000 in legal fees later, the asset purchase agreement was executed. For every concession Gifford Hill made, Merlin extracted a concession from Wales. By the time this transaction was closed, there was not a single management person at Wales that would speak to anyone at Gifford Hill, and the lawyers for both sides were intensely adversarial with each other. Merlin set the tone of the later negotiations by proposing a very unfair first draft and by his haughty attitude. This is not the way to practice law in my view. I was totally opposed to the unnecessarily adversarial nature of negotiating this deal.

Merlin was incredible. He humiliated his subordinates. His treatment of me and other associates was unmerciful. He was intensely argumentative and outright rude to most people. In 1979, he made over $600,000 practicing law, but he refused to buy cigarettes that he smoked continuously. Instead, he relied on his secretary and me to supply his tobacco habit. A typical illustration of Merlin's attitude involved his request that I give him all of the American Airline AAdvantage miles that I earned on trips for Mostek, so that Merlin could use them personally. Merlin was a director of Mostek and the reason why our firm was representing that company. Mostek paid for the flights we took, and at the time the AAdvantage miles were transferable. Merlin planned to take his wife and three children on a ski vacation, and he wanted the AAdvantage miles I had earned on trips I had taken at Mostek's expense. I told him that I would give them to Mostek, but I would not give them to him. He was furious. In a strange way, I think Merlin admired my sense of fairness and unwillingness to be pushed over by him. He ran over most people, including most lawyers.

While I worked for Merlin, we celebrated Kipp's first birthday. I will never forget Kipp simply jumping into his birthday cake with both feet. Six months later, he and I were planting a yaupon holly tree on the north side of our yard at our new home on Windy Meadow. I had dug a wide and deep hole, but when I dropped the tree into the hole, it went in sideways. I said "son of a bitch." For the next six months, Kipp walked around the house, echoing my "son of a bitch" every time something went wrong. I brought Kipp to the office one Saturday, and he got lost. Actually, he got on the elevator on the 23rd floor and rode it down to the first floor. The security guard brought him back safely.

During this time, Laura started taking classes at the Montessori Academy in north Dallas. This was a wonderful experience for her. Before she was five, she knew the shape of every state in the country, and she could name and spell each state and each capital city. She could add, subtract, multiply and divide some numbers. She could read at the third grade level. She absolutely loved her teacher, Ann Edwards, who she kept in touch with for many years after we left Dallas.

On January 2, 1979, Claudia and I were expecting to close the purchase of our third house in Dallas located at 4345 Edmondson in Highland Park. We left Tulsa at 2 p.m. on December 31, anticipating a leisurely drive to Dallas. Forty-five minutes into the drive an incredible ice storm hit. The normal four-hour trip to Dallas ultimately took more than 25 hours of driving. I skidded off the road once going 15 mph and could not stop. Eighteen-wheel trucks littered the ditches along the way. The ice was so bad that driving on the highway involved negotiating potholes where the ice had been stripped away, and cakes of ice remained on the highway. This was a scary and unbelievable experience. We closed the purchase of the house at 4:30 p.m. on January 2. For the next seventeen months, we had one remodeling project after another ongoing at the house. My angels protected me and my family from physical harm during that trip to Dallas.

The people that sold the house to us had lived there for more than twenty-five years. He was an alcoholic, and she was a terrible housekeeper. They owned two German Shepherds, and even kept goats and chickens in the backyard, even though the house was in the middle of Highland Park, the most prestigious part of Dallas. Simply cleaning up the house was an incredible chore. Building a neat playhouse in the back, however, was really fun. Both Laura and Kipp enjoyed playing in the playhouse.

Leaving Worsham Forsythe & Sampels

Around Thanksgiving 1979, I responded to a *Wall Street Journal* ad in which Hall Estill, Hardwick, Gable, Collingsworth & Nelson in Tulsa was seeking a corporate and finance lawyer. In late January 1980 I was in Tulsa taking depositions in the Texas interconnection case. We finished around 3 p.m., and I called Hall Estill to say that I was in town. I got an offer on the spot at a salary of $50,000, which was my salary in Dallas the prior year. I expected to make at least $75,000 at Worsham Forsythe in 1980. I neither accepted nor rejected the Hall Estill offer.

Four months later, my law school roommate and Beta pledge brother, John Toland, announced his engagement and plans to be married in Miami, OK in late May. John asked me to be an usher in his wedding. Claudia and I drove to Miami for the rehearsal on a Friday in late May, drove from Miami to Tulsa that evening to spend the night with my mother, and spent Saturday looking for houses in Tulsa just for fun. Saturday morning, Claudia walked into our current home at 1628 East 36th Court in Tulsa and said, "This is my house." I responded, "Let's buy it," which was the last thing on my mine.

After John's wedding Saturday evening, Claudia and I returned to Tulsa that night. We looked at more houses on Sunday, and before leaving Tulsa, we made an offer to purchase the house on 36th Court. Our offer was $20,000 below the asking price. Our offer was subject to financing, and I knew that I could not arrange financing unless we sold our house in Highland Park. Mortgage rates were down from 21% to about 12.5%, but still I knew that I could not finance the purchase of the Tulsa house unless we were able to sell our Dallas home. On Monday morning, our lowball offer was accepted. That afternoon I listed our Dallas home for sale. Eight days later, a young couple made an offer to buy our Dallas home with no financing contingency. The husband's father was president of the Texas Savings & Loan Association and could finance his son's purchase of our home in Dallas without bank financing.

Upon acceptance of our purchase offer for the Tulsa house, I called Hall Estill to inquire whether the job they offered me four months earlier was still available. It was, so I accepted. I said I would report on June 30, the day before a new plan year started under their employee benefit programs.

My time at Worsham Forsythe was incredibly difficult and interesting. I was determined to succeed, however, despite Merlin Sampels' unpleasant treatment of everyone. I had become a partner in the firm on January 1, 1980, but I was not happy billing 275 hours a month on average and working even more than that. I also could not see myself moving to Washington, DC for two to three years to try the Comanche Peak operating license case before the NRC. Once again, angels surrounded my move to Tulsa and carried me to a position with new challenges and new excitement in Tulsa.

Hall Estill
1980-1986

We moved to Tulsa in June 1980, just before my Edison high school class hosted its nineteenth class reunion. I was pleased to be able to show off Claudia, Laura and Kipp. I started work at Hall Estill in late June.

Agrico's Louisiana Sales Tax

My first assignment at Hall Estill was to consider a proposed Louisiana state sales tax upon the sale of ammoniated fertilizer produced by Agrico in Louisiana for sale in international commerce, primarily to China. At the time, Louisiana had an incredible 26% unemployment rate, and the state was scrambling for revenues from any possible source. There were fifteen other major petrochemical companies in Louisiana producing ammoniated fertilizers for shipment in international commerce. The proposed tax against Agrico amounted to approximately $10 million a year. For the industry, the total was approximately $50 million annually. The industry was united in an effort to launch a lobbying campaign to amend the statute to specifically exempt their products from state sales tax. I believed that the statute on its face did not subject any of these companies to taxation, and I believed that a legislative effort would not be successful in the face of the 26% employment and could undermine the position that the law as written could not reach sales for resale.

I conducted a survey of state sales and use tax laws and cited numerous judicial decisions stating that the sales and use tax did not apply to sales of products made for resale. Based upon my memo, Agrico took the position that no lobbying effort was necessary. Ray Kelly, my supervisor, read the memo. His only comment was that I should at least get the name of the client correct. My memo started with "Agrico Chemical Corporation," when in fact the name of the client was "Agrico Chemical Company." I never forgot that lesson. My position prevailed in litigation, but I was never credited with that position from anyone within Hall Estill for saving Agrico and other petrochemical industry participants more than $50 million in state sales taxes annually.

North Carolina Phosphate Company

Agrico sold more than a $1 billion a year of ammoniated fertilizers. These fertilizers were produced from natural gas, phosphate and sulfur. One of the largest known deposits of phosphate in the world is located near Morehead City, North Carolina. Agrico and Kennecott Corporation had aggressively purchased mineral leases in this phosphate deposit for several years. Agrico conceived of building a world scale phosphate mining operation by entering into a series of joint ventures with large foreign users of ammoniated fertilizer products. Agrico would contribute its phosphate reserves and would build and operate the phosphate mines, while the foreign joint venture partners would make a large cash capital contribution to fund building the mines and would sign long-term take-or-pay supply contracts. It was estimated that the phosphate mined would cost approximately $450 million, that another approximately $50 million would be needed to build a deep water port at Morehead City and that an additional $38 million would be spent on barges for use at the port.

Stan Betzer, one of the smartest lawyers I have ever met, had overall responsibility for NCPC project under the direct supervision of Ray Kelly. I was hired to assist Stan in negotiating the joint venture arrangements with BASF, a $25 billion German petrochemical company, and with Albright & Wilson, a huge British subsidiary of Tenneco, while Stan worked on similar arrangements with the French and Italian governments and with major Japanese trading companies. I was also charged with negotiating the port agreement with Morehead City Port Authority and in structuring, negotiating and financing the acquisition of the ocean going barges.

Our negotiations with BASF took me to their headquarters in Germany, where a senior vice president of Agrico and I spent a week negotiating a joint venture arrangement with a committee of twenty-five principals and lawyers representing BASF, which we consummated. To celebrate, we spent a weekend in Paris and flew the Concorde back to Dallas. Later, a long-term lease of port facilities was signed, along with a port construction and operating agreement at Morehead City Port. These efforts proved unnecessary. Agrico was sold, and the NCPC project was never built.

Kennecott Closing

The NCPC project led me to lawyer the purchase of substantial phosphate mineral reserves owned by Kennecott Corporation in North Carolina for a cash purchase price of $164 million. On Thursday one week before Thanksgiving, I was asked by C. J. Head, general counsel of The Williams Companies, to draft a simple asset purchase agreement and related closing documents. The following Tuesday I accompanied Mr. Head and Bob Gwynn, the chairman of Agrico, to Greenwich, CT, to meet with Kennecott. I will never forget the treatment shown to us at Kennecott headquarters. The three of us were put in a room at 1 p.m. in the afternoon, given no food or water or other refreshments and basically ignored for the first ten hours we were there.

The Kennecott lawyers were mean-spirited, adversarial and incredibly rude. Mr. Head came to Connecticut to close the deal, and he would not allow their behavior to interfere with closing that deal. We negotiated all day and throughout the night on Wednesday, successfully consummating the purchase agreement at 9 a.m. Thanksgiving morning. Arrangements had been made with Chemical Bank to make the $164 million cash purchase price available to Kennecott on Thanksgiving Day. After confirmation of receipt of the funds, we flew on The Williams Companies' jet back to Tulsa. They dropped me off in Wichita, Kansas, so that I could join Claudia and the kids for Thanksgiving in Pratt, KS.

CO_2 Project

Agrico owned and operated a natural gas processing and ammoniated fertilizer manufacturing facility in Vertigris, OK, at the end of the Kerr-McClellan waterway. Large quantities of CO_2 are produced in processing nitrogen and simply vented into the air as a by-product. CO_2 is a colorless, odorless, non-toxic gas that disburses in the air without any danger to the environment. CO_2 is called "dry ice" in solid form. Liquid CO_2 is used in a variety ways, including fast-freezing poultry and enhancing oil and gas production. Bill Loyd, an Agrico business development officer, envisioned liquefying the CO_2 at the Vertigris plant and selling it on a long-term, take-or-pay agreement.

Bill's idea was to create a joint venture with an industry partner. Agrico would capture the 3,200 tons of CO_2 produced daily at the Vertigris plant, liquefy it and sell it to the industry partner on a long-term take-or-pay agreement. Liquid Carbonics of Chicago agreed to be that joint venture participant. My task was to prepare the joint venture agreement, the CO_2 liquefaction construction agreement, an operating agreement and the $8 million tax exempt bond financing documents to finance the project.

During one trip to Liquid Carbonics' headquarters in Chicago, Bill Loyd and I had dinner at a restaurant where the waitresses and waiters were want-to-be professional singers, dancers or actors. Bill discovered that our waitress was also an astrologer. She charged $10 to provide a palm reading and astrological chart. I thought the whole thing was a joke, but I finally agreed to give her $10 at Bill's urging in response to a "double dare" bet with Bill that we would never hear from her again. About two weeks later, I received a nine-page handwritten astrological reading which nailed me to a T. On top of the astrological chart was a two-page typewritten collection of scriptural verses, prepared by my secretary (whose husband was a Rhema Bible student), denouncing reliance upon stargazers and astrologists. This was the only paper that my secretary typed while she was employed by Hall Estill that did not contain numerous typographical, spelling and grammatical errors.

The CO_2 liquefaction plant was constructed on time, within budget and paid for itself within eleven months. The long-term contract with Liquid Carbonics was for twenty-five years. In the process of completing this deal, Bill Loyd and I became lifelong friends. We even organized a tennis and bridge supper group with two other couples, Cathy and Dwight Rychel and Cathy and Joe Craft, in which for more than two years, the four couples would set aside one Saturday evening a month to play tennis, have dinner at the home of one couple of the group and finish the evening off with two or three rubbers of bridge. The group disbanded when Bill and his family moved to North Carolina and Cathy and Dwight divorced.

FCD Oil

The early 1970s saw the price of oil and gas increase significantly. National energy policy gave tax benefits to domestic oil and gas producing companies. Almost everybody in Tulsa made investments in oil and gas programs, usually in the form of oil and gas limited partnership interests, where the organizer of the limited partnership was the general partner and the investors were limited partners who enjoyed extensive pass-through tax benefits. Monte Ryle of FCD Oil in Enid became a significant client of Hall Estill when FCD Oil sought to raise money for oil and gas drilling programs. I was asked to prepare the private offering memoranda, which FCD Oil used to raise $6 to $10 million in each of several offerings.

Two significant legal developments occurred which facilitated these oil and gas investments. First, the SEC adopted Regulation D, which drew a bright line in defining a "private placement," making it far easier to determine that the offering was exempt from securities registration. Under Rule 506 of SEC Regulation D, the issuer could sell to an unlimited number of accredited investors and to no more than 35 persons who did not qualify as accredited investors. Second, Regulation D clarified the law with respect to what constituted a single private offering by codifying the "integration" concept. If two or more offerings occur at approximately the same time for essentially the same purpose with an investment in the same type of security for the same type of consideration, then the offerings would be "integrated" into a single offering to determine compliance with Regulation D.

Historically, oil and gas promoters had issued limited partnership interests in several partnerships a year, one after the other without describing where the money would be spent. These so called "blind pools" created a question as to whether the number of non-accredited investors in previous drilling programs must be counted in determining if Regulation D was complied with. If they were counted, then both of the offerings with a combined number of more than 35 non-accredited investors would be unlawful. In response, the oil and gas industry shifted to "identified prospect" fundraising, where extensive geological information for each specific proposed oil and gas well was required to be included in the private offering memorandums. Great care was taken to insure that each limited partnership offering was in strict compliance with Regulation D.

Regulation D did not disturb prior federal securities law concepts of "securities fraud," where it is a crime for an issuer of securities to include false or materially misleading information or to fail to disclose material information in connection with the offer or sale of securities. The private offering memorandums prepared for these oil and gas programs resembled prospectuses similar to what is included in registered public offerings. Typically, the offering document was printed at a financial printer with the offering memorandum numbered sequentially and carefully tracked.

State securities laws were monitored carefully to insure that all criteria were present for an exemption from registration at the state level as well as at the federal level. Working on FCD oil and gas offerings led me into close contact with Monte Ryle, which ultimately led me to lawyer the acquisition of Kaiser Steel Company.

Kaiser Steel

Prior to forming FCD Oil, Monte Ryle was involved in extensive efforts to acquire coal mining rights in southeastern Colorado and northeastern New Mexico. Because coal is a principal source for generating electric power, because massive coal deposits are located in Wyoming and Montana and because transportation of coal from Montana and Wyoming to south Texas is very expensive, developing coal reserves 500 miles closer to the south Texas electric generation plants produces a significant transportation cost savings and is a tremendous competitive advantage over Wyoming coal.

One of the most fascinating ideas I worked on was the construction a pipeline from southeastern Colorado to southern Texas. The notion was to pulverize coal into powder, and slurry the coal in a stream of CO^2 gas. The coal would be pulverized at the mining site.

Very plentiful streams of CO_2 in New Mexico and Colorado would move the coal to Texas, where the coal would be separated from the CO_2 and the CO_2 would be injected in the ground to enhance oil and gas production.

The largest owner of coal reserves west of the Mississippi was Kaiser Steel Company. Kaiser Steel used coal to fire its steel manufacturing facilities in Fontana, California. Imports of low cost steel from South America and Japan, increased labor costs in the United States and the adoption of extremely expensive environmental control requirements literally drove the US steel producers out of business.

A worldwide auction was conducted for the sale of the Kaiser Steel assets. Kaiser Steel had more than 500 matters in litigation, had an under-funded liability to its union medical plan benefits which exceeded $500 million, had extensive other potential liabilities, with more than 10,000 employees in unions demanding ever increasing labor and employment benefits. Kaiser's steel manufacturing facilities were old and inefficient, they would have violated many environmental rules had they not been grandfathered and the company was desperately in need of extensive capital improvements. A west Texas electric utility company approached Monte, offering to finance the acquisition of Kaiser, seeking to obtain access to Kaiser's coal reserves and the two coal mines owned by Kaiser in New Mexico.

Kaiser Steel also owned extensive real estate in California in the fastest growing area in the country. Kaiser enjoyed exemptions from numerous environmental requirements, because of its grand fathered position at Fontana.

Monte Ryle salivated over the Kaiser coal reserves in New Mexico. Joe Frates, a real estate developer in Tulsa, saw an opportunity to acquire the real estate holdings of Kaiser in California. I assisted Monte Ryle in executing a $2 billion twenty-five-year long-term coal supply agreement, which would provide the requirements for a new coal fired generation station. Monte believed that this long-term supply contract would be bankable, so that he could finance the $100 million to commence operations of a new coal mine in southeastern Colorado. Acquiring Kaiser would eliminate the need to spend $100 million to open a new coal mine, because Kaiser already operated two coal mines in New Mexico. Armed with this long-term coal supply contract and the oral financing commitment from the west Texas electric utility company, Monte threatened to commence a tender offer for Kaiser Steel.

While the Kaiser acquisition was pending, FCD Oil was rapidly running out of money to finance its oil and gas operations. In early December 1984, I was asked to prepare a new private placement for a year end oil and gas exploration program in which FCD would raise $10 million. With ten days' effort, the private offering memorandum was printed in final form and ready for use. There was no assurance that the Kaiser transaction would be completed and without the capital raised in this offering, FCD would be bankrupt. I listed the company's going concern as a risk factor on the front page of the private placement memorandum. Monte freaked out. He ordered me to remove the disclosures from the offering memorandum, which I refused to do. He then went to my boss, threatening to fire Hall Estill if we refused to remove these accurate risk factors from the offering documents. FCD Oil owed our firm over $350,000 in legal fees, which we would never receive if FCD went belly up.

A securities lawyer is often placed in a difficult task. There is constant tension between the marketing side of the offering, in which the client hopes to puff the investment to sell the deal, and the requirement for full, accurate, honest, concise, fair and materially complete disclosure of all material facts. Failure to present the offering in a positive light may mean that the offering would be unsuccessful, because investors may not catch the excitement of the deal. Failure to disclose all material information subjects the company to claims of securities fraud.

There are extensive ethical obligations on the part of the securities lawyer when management requires the lawyer to take an action which could result in the commission of securities fraud. The lawyer is required to take action to stop that effort. Those actions include verbal and written advice to senior management of the company, which, if unheeded, requires the lawyer to take the matter to the highest authority within the company, usually the board of directors. If the advice is not heeded, the lawyer either must withdraw from representation and/or report the potential criminal offense to enforcement personnel, including federal and state securities administrators.

The Oklahoma State Securities Administrator was David Newsome, a former lawyer at Hall Estill and one who had worked under my direction and supervision on oil and gas offerings prepared for FCD Oil during 1984. Consequently, he not only was familiar with FCD and Monte Ryle, but he was also intimately familiar with the financial condition of FCD. Had this year-end offering proceeded without accurate disclosures regarding the Kaiser Steel project and the unstable financial condition of FCD, there is no doubt that the Oklahoma Department of Securities would have taken enforcement action of some type.

Moreover, the law at the time was that lawyers and accountants who provided significant efforts to facilitate securities offerings were themselves potential aiders and abettors in a securities fraud and were potentially subject to civil liability and potential criminal penalties.

It was imperative for FCD to complete a year-end offering to enable it to remain financially viable while the Kaiser transaction proceeded to consummation. The attitude of senior management at FCD Oil, the fact that FCD Oil owed Hall Estill almost $400,000 in fees with no ability to pay and the pressure from senior lawyers within Hall Estill to seek an accommodation with the client fell on my shoulders. There was no reasonable accommodation that I could make that permitted the client to proceed with the offering without extensive disclosures of its precarious financial condition. I was forced to take action.

Monte Ryle, who was the chairman and largest single shareholder of FCD Oil, refused to understand these issues. I was forced to notify his board and to require FCD to "stand down" or to provide complete accurate disclosure of these issues. Hall Estill and I were fired as counsel to FCD. An Oklahoma City firm simply picked up the offering documents that I drafted, deleted the risk factors and commenced the offering. The year-end offering was withdrawn before I notified enforcement agencies and my ethical crisis was avoided when FCD obtained a loan from one of its shareholders. Two weeks later, Hall Estill was re-engaged to assist FCD and its affiliates with the consummation of the Kaiser transaction. Once again, my angels were working overtime to protect me, to guide me and to keep me from harm.

The Kaiser acquisition group arranged a $100 million line of credit with City Bank and financing to discharge a major bond issue before the merger of Kaiser Steel into Kaiser Acquisition Corp. Extensive registration work with the SEC had to be finalized. Nevertheless, the $387 million cash merger agreement was consummated in March 1985. Monte Ryle became chairman of Kaiser Steel, and he asked me to be his general counsel in California. I declined. FCD ultimately paid all outstanding invoices from Hall Estill, as well as all fees earned and expenses incurred by Hall Estill in connection with the Kaiser acquisition. Two years later, Kaiser filed Chapter 11 bankruptcy, and extensive litigation naming Monte Ryle and others personally ensued.

Throughout this process, angels surrounded me and lifted me up when the pressures of the deal became almost unbearable. I am absolutely convinced that my actions were not only appropriate but were required under the circumstances. The legal positions taken by my client were untenable, factually inaccurate and legally unsustainable. I stood alone against the tide of pressure, both from within the law firm and from the client. I was strengthened by being correct. I went to extraordinary lengths to avoid the controversy. I sought every possible accommodation and corrective action short of a direct conflict with the client. Fortunately, my angels helped me stand tall under the pressure, and I became a better lawyer because of it.

Pawnee Industries

Pawnee Industries was acquired by an investment group led by the Sterling Group from Houston. Pawnee was a plastics manufacturer headquartered in Wichita, Kansas. The Sterling Group hired Burt Person of Tulsa to be president and chief executive officer. Burt was a 60 year old executive who had worked for three different companies in Tulsa that had gone public during his tenure. Burt's wife and the wives of two lawyers at Hall Estill had been part of a women's support group for more than ten years. Burt's employment termination by a Tulsa company and his subsequent alignment with the Sterling Group in the acquisition of Pawnee gave Hall Estill an opportunity to represent Pawnee over the next several years.

Within two months after the acquisition, I was asked by Jim Hardwick, a senior partner at Hall Estill, to resolve a management issue that jeopardized relations between Burt Person and the other board members at Pawnee. Under Section 83(b) of the Internal Revenue Code, a person receiving potential compensation through stock options vesting over time has the opportunity to elect in writing to be taxed on those benefits in the year in which the options are granted. The failure to make a timely election results in taxation of those benefits at the time the options were exercised.

When Burt joined Pawnee, he entered into a five-year employment agreement that entitled him to stock options that vested over a five year period. No Section 83(b) election was made. Because the strategic plan for Pawnee was to locate an acquisition target and take the company public, Burt's options had the potential of being extremely valuable, which would have resulted in a significant tax liability. In fact, within three months after the acquisition of Pawnee, the board of directors began to seek an investment banker to commence an initial public offering. To prepare for the public offering, the company recapitalized the outstanding stock by declaring a 2.6 shares per one stock dividend. Initial planning for the potential stock offering contemplated an offering price from $7 to $10 a share. The tax basis for shares held by members of the acquisition group after the stock dividend was less than $0.30 a share. Burt Person's initial $200,000 investment, combined with the vesting of his stock options, entitled him to almost 46% of the stock of the company, and his potential tax liability would have exceeded $1.5 million had no action taken place to resolve the Section 83(b) dilemma.

I recommended immediate vesting of all outstanding options with a third party appraisal valuing the shares at the time of vesting. Because of the transfer restrictions involved and the existence of a shareholders' agreement, which prohibited third party sales under most circumstances, the investment appraisal would be discounted by almost 40% of the value of the shares. The problem was that Burt would enjoy the benefit of significant increased ownership of Pawnee without having served time as president and without being an officer of the company to earn that right. The failure to make an 83(b) election, therefore, jeopardized the fundamental relationship between Burt and the other members of the board of directors.

After extensive deliberations, the board accepted my recommendation, fully vested all the options and permitted the immediate exercise by Burt of the options to which he was entitled under his employment agreement. The company paid the resulting income taxes to Burt, but the uneasy feeling between Burt and the other members of the board remained.

Within a year, I became unofficial general counsel for Pawnee. In that process Pawnee located an acquisition target, engaged lead underwriters for an initial public offering and prepared to file a registration statement that ultimately went effective at $7.50 a share. The Pawnee board meeting, which approved the filing of the registration statement, was held in Dallas. The board meeting adjourned at approximately 3 p.m., allowing me to race to the airport, fly back to Tulsa and coach Kipp's baseball team into a loss. I had my priorities straight, and the coaching decision I made was correct, but a perfect throw from center field to home plate nailed our runner at home plate, denying Kipp's team a victory which would have sent it to the city championships. Where were my angels that afternoon?

Pornographic Closing Documents

One of my strangest transactions involved the sale of Agrico's 50% interest in a phosphate mining operation in Brazil to its Brazilian joint venture partner for $25 million in cash. With extensive coordination between me and local Brazilian counsel, we scheduled a closing on Wednesday afternoon in New York City. Because of local currency regulations in Brazil, all of the bank documents had to be physically executed in San Palo, Brazil, and forwarded from Brazil to New York to consummate the closing. Two large conference rooms in a major New York City law firm were used to lay out the closing documents. By Wednesday afternoon, the transaction was pre-closed, and the parties simply had to wait receipt of the documents from Brazil, which were scheduled to arrive early Thursday morning.

After waiting all day Thursday, we were informed by buyer's counsel that technical difficulties prohibited a Thursday closing. That night I saw my first Broadway show, A Chorus Line. On Friday, we finally learned what had happened. Our closing documents were placed on the aircraft for shipment to the United States in a container filled with pornographic films. US Customs agents would not let the documents past customs. After almost two days' effort, the customs officials finally released the closing documents, and we were able to close around 3:00 p.m. on Friday.

Lawyers Galore

I experienced many transactions in which too many lawyers threatened consummation of the transaction. The most egregious of those transactions was the potential formation of a significant independent oil and gas company that planned to consolidate oil and gas properties held by three diverse ownership groups under the leadership of John Brock of Houston, TX. My client owned approximately $23 million in oil and gas properties located all over the Southwest. Two publicly traded companies headquartered in Denver also owned oil and gas properties having a value of approximately $23 million. John Brock was a prominent oil and gas businessman in Houston with extensive contacts within the industry and with tremendous credibility and charisma. He was president of the Houston Petroleum Club and his investors included Boone Pickens and John Connolly and many other prominent Texas oilmen.

Jim Hardwick and I from Tulsa met with the Houston lawyers at Vincent Elkins representing John Brock and the Houston lawyers at Baker & Botts representing the Denver public companies. The Denver public companies were controlled by First Reserve Corporation, which was headquartered in Stanford, CT and managed extensive pension and profit sharing funds for numerous public and private unions. Our client had two lawyers and one principal from Tulsa. John Brock had eleven lawyers and one principal from Houston. The Denver group had seven lawyers and two principals from Stanford.

The Vincent Elkins lawyers consisted of a senior partner, two mid-level partners, three young partners and several associates of varying degrees of experience. The billing rate for Vincent Elkins lawyers and Baker & Botts on an hourly basis exceeded $5,000 an hour. Vincent Elkins agreed to take the lead in drafting the asset purchase agreement. The initial asset purchase agreement was so poorly written that it did not even correctly identify the assets to be contributed or the names of the parties. I had to completely revise all of the documents.

During preliminary due diligence, I discovered that Brock Oil was the general partner in a number of oil and gas investment partnerships, including one which had drilled a deep gas well in Mississippi. Unfortunately, the drilling stem was lost in the hole, and the well was a blow out, resulting in several million dollars in damages and extensive personal injuries. As general partner of the partnership, Brock Oil was liable for the debts of the partnership. The proposed consolidation of Brock Oil with the other properties was doomed, unless there was a structural way to isolate the liabilities of Brock Oil from this new transaction. Several proposals were made to accomplish this result, but the principals never got comfortable that legal structuring could sufficiently protect their interests. The transaction never closed.

Several lessons were learned from this experience. Negotiation by committee is extremely expensive, requires extensive coordination and is unwieldy, if not impossible. There was absolutely no reason to have eleven lawyers from Vincent Elkins and seven lawyers from Baker & Botts in the preliminary meetings leading up to the possible acquisition. Lawyering by committee is a common problem when clients hire large law firms. Finally, careful due diligence can prevent horrible consequences. Had we not discovered the Mississippi blowout, the liabilities associated with that blowout would have contaminated the new venture and could ultimately have destroyed any possibility for its success and even jeopardized the continued viability of the parties.

Petromark

Petromark Resources was a small independent oil and gas exploration company whose owners consisted of John Williams, Chairman of The Williams Companies; Larry Bump, Chairman of Wilbros

Energy; and Larry Sandel, senior corporate lawyer at Hall Estill and others. Petromark grew out of an opportunity for senior executives at Williams to make personal investments when their companies declined to take advantage of those opportunities. Tom Campbell was president, and John Briggs was vice president and a lawyer.

Petromark identified Ike Lovelady, Inc. as a possible reorganization target. That firm had successfully consummated three oil and gas drilling limited partnerships, raising approximately $50 million in the process. When the exploration efforts proved unsuccessful, the investors in these programs sued. Ike Lovelady filed for protection under Chapter 11 of the Bankruptcy Code and sought to reorganize. Petromark became the proponent of a plan of reorganization pursuant to which Petromark would acquire the Ike Lovelady properties without the associated debts, the securities fraud claims filed by investors in those programs would be discharged and related bank debt would be restructured. Ike Lovelady acted as a debtor in possession and engaged a large bankruptcy firm in Fort Worth to represent it. I represented Petromark in the proposed reorganization.

The plan of reorganization contemplated taking Petromark public by way of the bankruptcy court, discharging most of the indebtedness of Ike Lovelady and acquiring the valuable oil and gas properties of Ike Lovelady free of prior debt. Time was of the essence. Larry Sandel, senior corporate lawyer at Hall Estill, was not only a significant personal investor but also was a director of Petromark.

After waiting over two months to receive a draft of the plan of reorganization from Lovelady's counsel in Fort Worth, an ultimatum was given that we would come to Fort Worth on a Friday if the draft was not provided. Thursday afternoon, we received a seventy-page draft plan of reorganization that did not even contain the proper names of the parties and was so unprofessionally written that it defied logic.

Upon our arrival in Fort Worth the next morning at 11:00 a.m., John Blenn, the senior partner of the bankruptcy firm and a former bankruptcy judge, met with us for a few minutes and then left us in a conference room until 6:00 p.m. I recommended that we completely rewrite the plan of reorganization and discard the work that was done by the Fort Worth firm. John Briggs and I asked for two secretaries to stay with us Friday evening and into the night, and at 8:00 a.m. the following morning, a new plan of reorganization was written and ready for mailing to the creditors. All that was required of Fort Worth counsel was to sign the cover letter, which I also prepared.

This plan of reorganization was approved virtually unanimously by the creditors and not changed by the bankruptcy court. It was also reviewed and approved by the SEC. The Petromark reorganization closing took an entire week to complete. The three securities fraud cases were resolved. The extensive financing required to complete the closing was funded. The reorganization was documented, and Petromark's stock became publicly traded through the bankruptcy process.

The Fort Worth law firm submitted an invoice for services and expenses in the amount of approximately $479,000. Their fee application contained time sheets for every one of the twenty lawyers in the firm who had worked on the matter. The day before the hearing to confirm the plan of reorganization, two lawyers from this Fort Worth firm came to Dallas Sunday afternoon and spent from 2:00 p.m. to 8:00 p.m. in meetings to coordinate the confirmation hearing on Monday morning. One of the lawyers slept for five of the six hours he was in the room. He billed twenty-six hours to the file on the date.

In essence, the fee application grossly overstated the amount of fees earned. The parties ultimately settled the fee application for approximately $250,000, and that amount was grossly overstated. I should have filed a grievance complaint against those lawyers. No wonder clients get upset with lawyers and law firms over billing matters!

The Petromark reorganization case gave rise to a significant conflict between me, who acted as lead lawyer on the case for Petromark, and Larry Sandel, a member of the board of directors of Petromark.

Larry refused to disclose to me the substance of meetings of the board of directors of Petromark, many of which had potential disclosure ramifications in the documents filed with the SEC.

This matter represented the classic case in which a lawyer was a member of a law firm and also a member of a board of directors for a client, where the client owed the law firm over $250,000 in fees and where significant material conflicts of interest permeated the entire file. I was pressured to consummate the reorganization. I was legally obligated to present a correct, accurate and materially honest disclosure statement upon which the creditors of Petromark could make informed investment decisions, and I was the lead lawyer responsible to the client for consummating the deal.

At the same time, Petromark would not and could not fund the legal fees required to complete this transaction unless the reorganization was completed as consummated. As a securities lawyer, I was potentially exposed personally for inaccuracies or inadequacies of disclosure had there been any, all of which would have been the direct result of my own partners' refusal to provide me information with respect to matters discussed at the board of directors level. In my view the situation was absolutely unacceptable, and I expressed that view to management at Hall Estill.

The situation was complicated, because Larry Sandel was simply not around most of the time during this process. His personal problems could have affected adversely the firm's ability to consummate the transaction and could have exposed the firm and me to significant litigation and potential personal liability.

Moreover, my principal contact at Petromark was Tom Campbell, the president. Conflicts had arisen between Tom and members of the board of directors over his leadership and over specific decisions. The day following the closing, I was re-assigned to other duties and another lawyer in the firm was assigned to represent Petromark. Thank God!

Buying 727s

My client, Stan Bernstein, agreed to buy three 727 jet aircraft from South African Airways, a government-owned airline. He planned to resell those planes to a predominantly black African nation neighboring South Africa. Apartheid prevented a direct sale. The plan was to finance the purchase with a major Japanese bank headquartered in New York using Swiss Francs as the currency and using LIBOR (London InterBank Offering Rate) interest. This was a real law school exam dilemma. Stan Bernstein's personal lawyer and accountant, Jack Schuler, assisted me.

We boarded Ozark Airlines in Tulsa as it began to snow about 3:00 p.m. one mid-January afternoon en route to LaGuardia in New York City. We flew to St. Louis for our connecting flight. It was really snowing in St. Louis when we landed. Just as we were boarding our flight to New York City, the news media flashed the story of an airplane that slid off the end of the runway at Washington National Airport right into the Potomac River. Numerous tales of heroism followed, with a movie later being made of this event. The cause was icing on the wings. We boarded our flight and sat on the tarmac in St. Louis for one hour and forty-five minutes in delays.

As all passengers became more frustrated and as the snow continued to fall, the pilot announced over the intercom: "Good evening ladies and gentlemen. I apologize for the delay, but we are first for take off. We are allowed to take off because of a new change in FAA regulations. The old rules required that there be an airport available for landing before any takeoff. That requirement has been deleted. All the airports on the East Coast and in New England are now closed because of the weather, including LaGuardia and Kennedy, but we believe that LaGuardia will be open when we get there. Also, that airplane that slid off the runway at National did so because of icing on the wings. We have taken precautions by spraying our wings, but sometimes that spray just is not too effective. Relax and have a nice flight." Virtual mutiny ensued, but we still took off.

We flew into New York on the smoothest flight there ever. New York City was so beautiful as we flew over the city. We landed at LaGuardia, only to learn that the airport had been closed all evening and that we were the only flight to land in more than three hours. The snow plows were working feverishly piling eight to ten feet of snow along the tarmac.

When we got off the plane at 12:30 a.m., LaGuardia was entirely deserted. There was not a soul in sight, not even the cleaning people. This was the strangest feeling. There were always throngs of people in LaGuardia. More amazingly, there were no taxis and no cars in the parking lot. I saw a limo about 300 yards away from the terminal. I put my bags down and ran to see if we could get a ride. I asked the driver if he was going downtown. He said $50. I said I would pay $20. He said "$25 each." I said "Deal."

Jack and I rode in the front seat of the limo, me next to the driver, holding a woman with a lampshade on her lap and Jack with another woman on his lap holding a caged canary. The limo driver packed twenty people in the car, and drove 85 mph all over Manhattan, dropping off all the passengers at their homes. We were the last to be dropped off at the Madison Hotel at about 1:45 a.m., across from Central Park in Midtown Manhattan. What a trip! Angels provided us warmth and protection on that wild adventure.

The next morning, Jack and I pre-closed the purchase of the first of three 727s, anticipating a closing the following day. In order for title to a plane to be transferred, it must be de-registered from one jurisdiction and registered in another. Because there is an eight-hour time difference between South Africa and New York City, Jack expected to receive a telegram at about 6:00 a.m. At 5:30 a.m., Jack was awakened by a knock at his door. Jack opened the door, and a woman dressed as a "maid" and a huge black man rushed into the room, took Jack's Rolex, which his wife had given him years before, all his money, all his credit cards and all of his papers. They left within thirty seconds.

Jack called to tell me what happened. I invited him to meet me for breakfast. We went next door for a Danish and coffee, which cost $15 each. Jack wore his Russian styled fur hat and top coat, which he checked at breakfast. When we rose to leave, Jack discovered that someone had stolen his hat. He left the restaurant and within twenty steps Jack slipped on the ice and bruised his hip. The closing was a breeze after all that. During the closing, I used lots of 3M post-its. The Japanese had never seen post-its before. You could see them trying to figure out how to make them in Japan. What an ordeal!

Leaving Hall Estill

My departure from Hall Estill, as my departure from Jackson Walker and Worsham Forsythe and my other firms, was an adventure. In 1975, The Williams Companies, which accounted for more than 80% of the annual billings of Hall Estill, made a tender offer for Northwest Energy. Northwest Energy was headquartered in Salt Lake City, UT, but it owned a natural gas pipeline previously owned by Cities Service Pipeline of Tulsa, which Williams coveted. In fact, two years earlier, Williams tried to purchase that pipeline but lost in a bidding war with Northwest Energy. Hall Estill grew into the largest law firm in Oklahoma, because of The Williams Companies' determination not to hire its own in-house legal staff.

In the process of Williams acquiring and assimilating Northwest Energy, several things of significance to Hall Estill occurred. First, C. J. Head, a very good friend of Hall Estill and the general counsel of Williams, was spread so thin that he was unable to service his client.

Second, as part of the Northwest Energy acquisition, Williams acquired a twelve person in-house legal staff. The Williams Companies had historically not utilized in-house counsel, because their rates from Hall Estill were significantly discounted below market, Williams was not required to hire or fire in-house lawyers, and Williams was not required to pay the employee burden, which was approximately 45% to 50% of base compensation to house counsel. Moreover, Williams believed that it was unable to obtain quality lawyers for in-house positions.

Third, the president of Cities Service Pipeline, which was acquired in the Northwest Energy acquisition, became executive vice president and then president of Williams. He had grown up with a large in-house staff, which he viewed as the corporate norm. One of his first official actions was to engage Arthur Young's New York office to conduct a survey of the quality, cost and efficiency of the legal services provided by Hall Estill. Moreover, Agrico Chemical Company, which had produced a large portion of the annual gross revenue of Williams and Hall Estill, was on the auction block.

At the same time, the shareholders at Hall Estill with the longest longevity at the firm circulated a proposed revision to the share-holders' agreement, which tied voting rights to longevity with the firm, ensuring that the eight lawyers who were the most senior in longevity, when acting together, could control any decision at the firm, without regard to the desires of the other 40 shareholders. Anxiety at Williams resulted in fear at Hall Estill and caused Hall Estill's management to become greatly concerned over the direction and indeed survival of the firm.

One other factor that impacted this fear was the internal concerns raised by shareholders of the law firm. These concerns were triggered by disagreements with the positions taken by management in suggesting the new revision to the shareholders' agreement. Some of those included: (1) a concern over whether the firm's books should be audited, which Tom Gable, the managing partner, took as a personal insult and a direct assault on his integrity; (2) whether shareholders should have equal voice and equal votes in the selection of the board of directors and the executive committee, again flying squarely in the face of Tom Gable and his weighted longevity approach to shareholder management; (3) uncertainty as to the financial condition of the firm because of the Penn Square bank crisis and the fall out from the savings and loan crisis; and (4) the death of Fred Nelson, the senior litigator, and the struggle within the litigation group for control and management of the largest department in the firm.

These internal concerns developed into what management viewed as an insurrection at a monthly shareholders' meeting in November 1985 when Stan Betzer, Ed Norris and Ron Platner vocalized some of these concerns. Stan was the third senior lawyer in the corporate group and was in charge of the NCPC project, which had been placed on hold while Agrico was being auctioned. Ed Norris was a senior tax partner with oil and gas limited partnership and international tax practice experience. Each of those areas of Hall Estill's practice had significantly subsided, due to changes in tax laws and the general malaise in the investment community. Ron Platner was an outstanding tax and corporate lawyer, who had been assigned to work through a major limited partnership bankruptcy case for almost two years, but that case had settled.

A committee of five lawyers was appointed to collect suggestions for improvement in the firm and to bring the comments of all lawyers within the diverse departments in the firm into a single forum where those issues could be reported, discussed and managed. I was named secretary of this committee. I tried not to be on the committee, but most of the people liked and respected me and knew I would act honestly, whatever the consequences. I feared what actually happened. The senior management blamed the messenger, rather than looking to solve the problems identified, in February 1986, after studying the various issues and collecting numerous recommendations on how the firm could be improved.

I wrote the unanimous committee's report, which detailed all of the suggestions made and provided the committee's recommendations with respect to the implementation of some and the rejection of other suggestions, concerns and comments. Tom Gable and perhaps others viewed the report as an act of open insurrection by me, even though all I did was write down ideas expressed by others.

Three weeks after the report was provided to management of the firm, a vote along longevity lines was taken to adopt the shareholders' agreement in the form presented by management. No effort was made to implement any of the committee's suggestions. My efforts and the efforts of the committee to improve the firm were simply ignored. Instead, the senior management looked for ways to further entrench their positions.

A month later a memo from the board of directors, the only such memo issued in my six years at Hall Estill, announced that: "Three shareholders had decided to leave the firm. The board wishes them well." Speculation for at least six weeks thereafter concluded that Stan Betzer, Ed Norris and Ron Platner would be leaving involuntarily. These were three terrific lawyers with expertise in securities, international tax, limited partnership tax, bankruptcy taxation and corporate matters. The departure of these three lawyers left the firm with voids in those areas and with a very sour taste in the mouths of all the other shareholders. It was no coincidence that these three lawyers were the ones who vocalized concerns relating to an audit of the firm books, implementing one vote for each shareholder, and the unfair use of two condominiums purchased with firm money by a select group of older shareholders. The message was clear. Either shut up or you might be asked to leave.

Not only were these three terrific lawyers, but also these three lawyers were three of my best friends in the firm. Each of them secured positions with much better firms in other locations. Stan went to Albuquerque, NM, with the largest firm in that state. Ed Norris went to Los Angeles to establish a tax department for a major Wall Street law firm. Ron Platner went to Phoenix as a senior tax partner in a major developing law firm there. While I was not asked to leave or encouraged to even think about leaving by anyone in the firm, I concluded that if the management of the firm was so insecure and could disrupt the lives of these three superb lawyers, it could do it to me, and any one of us at any time, at its whim.

In April 1986, I decided to leave Hall Estill. Except for Claudia, however, I told no one of this decision. I spoke to no other lawyers at Hall Estill, and I spoke to no clients or employees of clients about my desire to represent them after my departure. While I continued to be paid by Hall Estill, I should be a loyal employee and do my very best representing clients of Hall Estill until I officially departed. Thereafter, these clients were fair game.

During the year prior to my departure from Hall Estill, one of the goals of the corporate department was to increase the number of 1934 Act reporting clients. Public companies with at least 500 shareholders and $1 million in assets were required to be registered, to file annual, quarterly and periodic reports with the SEC and to comply with the proxy rules. I was primarily responsible for securing three new public companies, Pawnee Industries, Petromark Resources and Florafax International.

In early May, Bill Lobeck of Thrifty Rent-A-Car called indicating that his franchisee in California desired to sell the franchise back to the company. I prepared an asset purchase agreement overnight and delivered it to Bill the following day, enabling Thrifty to make a strategic acquisition that ultimately led Thrifty to do an initial public offering. Tempo Enterprises was another target for Hall Estill. Several of us had preliminary contacts with Tempo, but it was Stan Betzer who met with Selman Kramer, Ed Taylor's right hand man, that led to my post-Hall Estill representation of Tempo. While Stan was one of the most capable lawyers I have ever known, he declined to work on securities matters, because he was not a "full-time" securities lawyer.

I had no such fear. Shortly before my departure from Hall Estill, I interviewed with Ed Taylor and the board of directors of Tempo, seeking Tempo as a Hall Estill client. On July 2, on the second day after my resignation from Hall Estill, I was asked to draft a registration statement, anticipating a $50 million offering for Tempo. Three days later, I completed an initial draft, which I presented to Tempo's board. Tempo's general counsel feared being swallowed up by Hall Estill, but he did not fear me as an individual lawyer.

Before leaving Hall Estill, I felt it incumbent upon me to complete two projects that were scheduled to close in mid-July for which I had primary responsibility. The first of those involved a public convertible debenture offering in which Pawnee Industries raised $12.5 million through a registered public offering. The second involved a $4 million private placement offering by Florafax. Both of these offerings closed on July 18, 1986.

My time at Hall Estill was both instructive and very positive. I liked the people very much, and I was excited about the opportunity to work on projects which might have a world impact, particularly projects like the NCPC project, which would bring fertilizer and food to third world countries. In the end, however, self-interest and greed prevailed over teamwork and mutual best interests. Within three months after my departure, twenty-six other lawyers, some shareholders and some associates, left Hall Estill. I did not talk with any of these lawyers about leaving the firm, either before or after I left.

Undoubtedly some of them left involuntarily, but many left of their own discretion. I was saddened mostly by the nonchalant attitude taken by persons who I thought were close friends. Ray Kelly, Jim Hardwick, Bob Curry and others kept quiet, kept a low profile and stayed out of the line of fire, despite our friendships. Only Bill Nay continued to be a close friend of mine after my Hall Estill days. I neither encouraged others to leave or stay. Rather I simply had no contact with them.

Numerous changes occurred within our family during my time at Hall Estill. We moved into the house at 1628 East 36th Court in

Tulsa, the home in which we still reside. Claudia began playing her violin with the Oklahoma Sinfonia and, on occasion, with the Tulsa Philharmonic and for others. Laura started school at Elliot Elementary, two blocks from our home, craving homework, only to find that she was far ahead of her classmates and needed to transfer to Holland Hall. Laura continued with dance classes, which led her into ballet where she performed two years, once as a mouse and once as an angel, in the Tulsa Ballet Company's *Nutcracker*. Kipp followed Laura to Holland Hall, where he began playing competitive sports, especially basketball and baseball. One of my passions and joys has been to watch Laura and Kipp develop and grow. I especially enjoyed coaching them during these early years of competitive sports.

Another defining moment occurred when our family joined First United Methodist Church on Christmas Eve, 1980. Less than a year later, I volunteered to assist the church in raising $2 million to pay off indebtedness incurred to construct the children's wing. John Williams, Jr. and I helped lead a successful completion of the $2 million church bond offering in less than two weeks, stabilizing the church's financial condition and stretching out its indebtedness over a ten-year period. My efforts on this church bond offering led me to write what I planned to be a law review article but which grew into a book, which included a 50 state survey of the state securities laws applicable to church bond offerings published by CCH Blue Sky Reporter.

The six years at Hall Estill gave me a significant base from which to practice law in Tulsa, to be selected to various committees with the Oklahoma and Tulsa County Bar Associations, to become a frequent continuing legal education speaker and to balance my professional activities with service on the Oklahoma Sinfonia board and other charitable institutions. Angels surrounded me, guided me, lifted me up and sustained my professional and personal development during this period. Thank God for my angels.

Baker Hoster
October 1986 through June 1992

In leaving Hall Estill, I anticipated that I would continue to be the outside general counsel for Pawnee Industries, Florafax, Thrifty Rent-A-Car, Scepter and Tempo. Close personal relationships with Burt Person at Pawnee and with Bill Lobeck and Jim Phillion at Thrifty, with Floyd Cox at Florafax and with Garney Scott at Scepter Industries, convinced me that I would be able to continue to keep these clients. Within a month after my departure from Hall Estill, however, it became clear that neither Pawnee nor Thrifty would continue to use me, both of which believed that it was essential that a major law firm be listed as its general counsel. Nevertheless, because I had close contact with these clients, several law firms in Tulsa contacted me to determine whether I would be interested in associating with their firm. One of those groups was Baker, Hoster, McSpadden, Clark & Rasure.

I joined Baker Hoster with great anticipation and real excitement. Upon my arrival, Baker Hoster became Baker, Hoster, McSpadden, Clark, Rasure & Slicker. The other five named partners had been partners at Conner & Winters in Tulsa before they left as a group to form Baker Hoster in 1986. The firm was small, intimate and committed to excellence and growth. My general corporate and securities practice complemented the banking, litigation and bankruptcy practice of the other partners. For the next six years, I enjoyed an excellent association with these other lawyers, whose professional goals and objectives were the same as mine.

Scepter Industries

My representation of Garney Scott and Scepter Industries, Inc. is an excellent illustration of how my angels watched over me. At the age of thirty-two, Garney Scott was clearly on the fast track at Alcoa Aluminum. He was plant manager of Alcoa's largest aluminum ingot plant located near Corpus Christi with over 3,800 employees reporting to him. His success resulted in his promotion at age thirty-five to vice president of Alcoa in charge of Alcoa's worldwide aluminum ingot manufacturing. Garney moved from Texas to Pittsburgh, PA, the headquarters of Alcoa. But Garney was a line officer, not a staff adviser. Quickly he became very uncomfortable in the headquarters of this major corporation. He was used to running his operations, making his own decisions and solving problems quickly and effectively. At the headquarters, he had to staff his recommendations through endless committees before anything was done.

Because of his efforts to acquire technology owned by International Metals Company in Sapulpa, OK, Garney was offered employment at IMCO, and he moved to Tulsa with promises of an equity ownership in the company, a right of first refusal if the three owners decided to sell IMCO and an extensive bonus arrangement. Two and a half years later, Garney came to see me to review his employment agreement.

While in Pittsburgh, Garney became well-acquainted with a paralegal in Alcoa's legal department. After tragic events in her life, Tricia moved to California. Garney sought Tricia's advice, with respect to counsel in Tulsa, when events began to go south for Garney in Sapulpa. Tricia checked Martindale Hubbell, seeking a woman lawyer with a California connection. Nancy Vaughn, an estate planner and probate lawyer at Hall Estill was a law graduate from USC. Nancy brought Garney Scott to me to review his employment agreement. From Pittsburgh to California to Sapulpa to Hall

Estill, this was the circuitous route by which my longest client relationship and a close personal relationship began. How fascinating!

Shortly before Garney's three-year employment agreement at IMCO was to expire, the three owners of IMCO commenced negotiations to sell the company to an investment group led by Merrill Lynch in violation of their oral promise to Garney to grant him a right of first refusal to purchase the company. Garney's employment agreement, however, was silent with respect to the right of first refusal. More than that, they promised him at least a 10% equity interest in the business, but the promise was not in writing. Garney's employment agreement did contain a very strong non-competition agreement, which in my view was void under Oklahoma law.

Garney agreed to remain at IMCO while IMCO consummated its sale to the Merrill Lynch venture capital fund. However, he agreed to stay only if IMCO agreed to allow him to explore opportunities to purchase a business of his own in the aluminum recycling industry. Garney went to Alumax, Inc., a privately-owned Japanese company operating in the US, and persuaded that company to sell its Bicknell, Indiana, aluminum recycling plant. A letter of intent was entered into pursuant to which a new company would be formed by Garney called Scepter Industries, Inc., which would purchase the land, equipment and other fixed assets of the Bicknell plant for $3 million.

The raw materials inventory, the finished goods inventory and the accounts receivable were specifically excluded from the purchase, and no liabilities or accounts payable were to be assumed. When Garney was unable to arrange financing and in an effort to secure a 10% finder's fee which the owners of IMCO had also promised Garney, Garney presented this acquisition opportunity to IMCO, but IMCO declined and specifically granted Garney its consent for him to complete this purchase for his own account, even though Garney continued to be employed by IMCO while it struggled to complete the sale of its business.

Garney had never owned his own business. At this time, many banks and other financial institutions were suffering by reason of the Penn Square bank failure in Oklahoma City. Consequently, despite extensive efforts seeking financing from over thirty financial institutions, Garney was unable to find bank financing to complete the acquisition of the Bicknell facility.

Through Garney's friendship with the chairman of Alcoa, who was a member of the board of directors at Pittsburgh National Corporation, one of the twentieth largest banks holding companies in the US, PNC's venture capital fund agreed to loan Garney $1 million for six months with a forfeiture provision if the loan was not paid on time. This commitment had fees and expenses approximating $600,000 over the six-month period. The loan agreement, security agreement and other financing documents prepared by PNC's Pittsburgh's lawyers consisted of almost four inches of paper and had several forfeiture provisions in the event of a default.

The balance of the $2 million in funding necessary to complete the acquisition was provided by Pechiney Metals, the largest aluminum-processing firm in France. Instead of extensive documentation, Pechiney simply sent Garney a two-line telex that Pechiney would loan Scepter Industries $2 million, provided Scepter agreed to pay Pechney back in metal over the next two years.

Three days before closing, IMCO threatened litigation against Garney and Scepter, alleging that the acquisition of the Bicknell facility was a violation of Garney Scott's fiduciary duty and a violation of the corporate opportunity doctrine. Officers and directors of corporations have a duty of loyalty, so that they are not permitted to take a personal financial benefit by reason of their special knowledge and position with a company, unless the officer or director discloses the opportunity to the company and the company declines to accept and complete the transaction. IMCO falsely asserted that Garney was in effect "stealing" the opportunity to buy the Bicknell facility in violation of the corporate opportunity doctrine, even though Garney presented this acquisition to IMCO with full disclosure of the details and IMCO specifically declined the opportunity and specifically granted Garney permission to pursue it. IMCO gave notice to Pechiney and PNC bank of its claim and wrongfully sought to kill the lending commitments made by those companies to Garney. IMCO's threats were false, but immediately after closing, Scepter filed suit against IMCO for attempting to interfere with these contracts.

Until a day before closing, the Bicknell acquisition was planned as a $3 million fixed asset purchase. The Bicknell facility outstanding accounts receivable was made up of approximately $3.5 million and raw materials, work in process and finished goods inventory in the form of aluminum ingot of approximately $3.5 million. Alumax urged Scepter to purchase the accounts receivable, because after closing these customers would become customers of Scepter. Alumax also encouraged Scepter to purchase the inventory to avoid requiring Alumax to remove the ingots from the Bicknell plant site. Garney did not have the additional $7 million, having struggled to finance the $3 million fixed asset purchase.

To honor the request of Alumax, Garney negotiated a purchase of the accounts receivable, which were from Reynolds Aluminum, Alcoa Aluminum and other major US corporations, and agreed to pay Alumax for these collected receivables in 180 days, provided Alumax guaranteed the collection of the receivables, which it was willing to do.

Virtually all the receivables were collected within ten days after the closing, thereby providing Scepter with almost $3 million in working capital, which it would otherwise not have been available to Scepter had it not purchased the receivables.

Garney also negotiated the purchase of all of the raw materials, work in process and finished goods inventory at approximately 85% of fair market value. It would have cost Alumax approximately 25% of fair market value to remove this inventory from the Bicknell plant site and to store it at another facility. Garney agreed to pay Alumax in 150 days. Within three days after closing, Garney sold all the finished goods inventory at approximately fair market value. Garney's creative financing continues to be a model for me in other acquisition and financing transactions.

In order to facilitate the closing, PNC's $1 million and the Pechiney's $2 million were wired to a local San Mateo, CA, bank early Friday morning and wired to Alumax Friday afternoon. The local bank lending officer and his wife were awarded a paid vacation for a week in Hawaii for generating the largest dollar amount of new business for the bank during the month, even though the funds were in the bank less than three hours.

The Bicknell closing was also interesting from an administrative point of view. Alumax was owned by a Japanese trading company and its US headquarters were located in San Mateo, just east of San Francisco. Alumax had beautiful offices with very little administrative staff. My secretary, Susan Frisby, typed the closing documents in Tulsa and faxed them to me in California for execution at the closing. Virtually all of the administrative and clerical efforts to complete this closing were completed in Tulsa by Susan, even though the closing actually took place in California. This was long before fax machines became commonly used and before the Internet.

One final interesting event occurred in this closing. In order to fund PNC's $1 million, PNC's Pittsburgh lawyers required that UCC financing statements be on file before funding. In order to ensure the perfection of PNC's security interests, the UCC financing statements were sent for filing at the Secretary of State's office in Indiana and in Oklahoma two days before closing. Unfortunately, the plane carrying the documents to Indiana flew into a massive snowstorm and crashed. The documents were destroyed, along with the lives of all people on board. Because we sent these papers two days before closing, we were able to duplicate this effort the next day and to complete the closing as scheduled.

In many ways this was a closing from hell. Threatened litigation by Garney's existing employers sought to interfere with extensive and creative efforts that were extremely difficult to arrange. Administrative complications and difficulties sought to derange the closing. Extreme documentation was required with respect to a portion of the financing from the venture capital firm. Garney's persistence, his good nature, his positive attitude and his creativity enabled a very difficult transaction to be consummated, despite enormous efforts to keep the closing from occurring. My angels were present at each step in the process.

As a footnote, Bicknell became the first of many jewels in the Scepter crown. Garney was able to complete the repayment of the receivables and inventory financing well in advance of the due date. After significant efforts, Garney was able to refinance the PNC loan. Garney's relationship with IMCO continued to deteriorate and resulted in two major pieces of litigation, both of which were won by Scepter. Scepter Industries has grown into a company with more than $100 million in annual revenue with manufacturing plants in Indiana, Tennessee, Texas and New York and with joint venture arrangements in France and Mexico. Garney's operations have resulted in my opportunity to lawyer four acquisitions, three tax-exempt bond financings and numerous bank financings. A warm personal relationship between me and Garney continues today. All of this was made possible because a female paralegal in California made a referral to a firm in Tulsa with a female lawyer who went to a California law school.

Pawnee Industries Again

The 1986 Tax Reform Act went into effect January 1, 1987. Even though Pawnee Industries had completed a subordinated debenture offering in July 1986, the elimination of long-term capital gains was about to deprive the owners of significant anticipated tax savings. As a result, Pawnee negotiated its sale to a new investment group led by Brian Klump, Larry Widmer and the Sterling Group of Houston. This effort resulted in the consummation of a public tender offer for all of Pawnee's outstanding public securities and the sale of Pawnee to this new financing group on December 24, 1986. In early January 1987, Brian Klump and Larry Widmer called me to see if I had an interest in representing Pawnee in the future. Hall Estill had represented the old Pawnee group in the tender offer, so that firm had a conflict in representing the new Pawnee. I was delighted to have the opportunity to work with Brian Klump, Larry Widmer and Pawnee again.

During the next several years, Pawnee acquired businesses in Minnesota, Kansas and Texas. Pawnee established a series of investment and acquisition criteria which included the nature of the business, the geographic location of the principal facilities, the nature and synergy of customers and suppliers, the extent to which the target complemented Pawnee's core business, the maturity and experience of the target's management, the quality of the employees, the price to be paid and a variety of other factors. The Grand Prairie, TX, acquisition met these acquisition criteria like a hand in a glove. Within a year after offering to purchase the Grand Prairie facility for $15 million, Pawnee consummated a purchase for $31 million, with $25 million financed through bank borrowings and a $5 million seller carry.

During the Saturday evening celebration of Pawnee's twenty-fifth anniversary at Key Stone, CO, where the members of its board and all the key managers and their wives were present, Pawnee learned of the opportunity to acquire the Grand Prairie facility, after losing a bidding war a year earlier. I was asked to draft a letter of intent for transmission at 8:30 a.m. the following morning. I wrote the letter of intent by hand in the closet of my hotel room, beginning at 3:00 a.m. I had the letter of intent typed by the hotel staff by 8:30 a.m. The resulting stock purchase agreement contemplated long-term supply agreements for both plastic products and color additives.

Each of these long-term purchase agreements represented annual revenues to Pawnee in excess of $30 million. The gross margins of the target company averaged just under 15%; Pawnee's gross margin averaged more than 25%. The difference would pay for the acquisition in less than three years. This acquisition took Pawnee from annual revenues of approximately $70 million to annual revenues of approximately $150 million.

Despite the perfect match in investment criteria, the Pawnee acquisition of the Grand Prairie facility proved to be the death of Pawnee for three reasons. First and most significantly, the corporate culture within Pawnee and the target company were totally adverse. Pawnee was a privately-held, profit-driven company that maximized gross margins and bottom line profits. The Grand Prairie facility had historically been a third-tier subsidiary of Quaker Oats, Coca-Cola, Anderson Clayton and other major corporations. Instead of being profit-driven, Grand Prairie's management was left alone so long as they made a small profit.

Second, the former president, the national sales vice president, the entire marketing staff and the whole customer service group defected and went to work for a direct competitor down the street. In the process, these defecting employees took with them valuable customer relationships and confidential information about Pawnee and its pricing strategies. Pawnee lost about $35 million in business on an annual basis. The defecting employees also allegedly stole corporate records and computer files containing proprietary information relating to projected customer sales listed by product and priority and information relating to supply costs, which essentially delivered to Pawnee's principal competitor all of the financial and customer data necessary to steal those customers, which Spartech did.

Third, the Grand Prairie plant owned about 70% of the business nationally of a specific product group, and it enjoyed a national reputation for excellence and quality control with respect to all its products. The principal raw material supplier for this product group was Dow Chemical Company. Dow Chemical was also a major supplier to Pawnee. Dow Chemical had constructed a $100 million processing plant for the purpose of producing the raw materials used to manufacture marbelized plastic spas. Dow changed the specifications used in formulating the resins for this product. The result was a significant decline in quality. After several years of attempting to resolve those quality issues, Dow made a corporate decision to cease producing that raw material product. Pawnee was unable to replace that raw material with a compatible raw material with superior quality. Pawnee lost this business because there was no acceptable alternative material.

Ultimately, the litigation resulting from the wholesale departure of all the Pawnee management team of the Grand Prairie facility and its defection to a competitor, the loss of quality in the marbelized spa product line, the significant difference in corporate culture and the inability to service the acquisition debt led to the sale of the Grand Prairie facility for less than $2 million and the ultimate sale and dismemberment of Pawnee. The predatory practice engaged in by Spartech which engineered the departure of the Grand Prairie management led to four years of litigation against Spartech and a nine-week bench trial in which Pawnee sought $35 million in actual damages, together with punitive damages. Spartech's anti-competitive practices continued during trial, which resulted in numerous sanctions for discovery abuses and lies by numerous Spartech witnesses. Still, Pawnee lost.

Sexual Harassment at Pawnee

Long before the Clarence Thomas Supreme Court nomination elevated sexual harassment in the workplace to national attention, claims of sexual harassment were made within the Pawnee organization. The first allegation of significance was that a production line worker at its Paulding, OH, manufacturing facility claimed sexual harassment by her supervisors. In truth and in fact, this claimant voluntarily and consensually submitted to repeated events of a sexual nature. The former owner of Pawnee owned a condominium in Paulding, which was used often by supervisors and employees for sexual purposes when the owner was not present. Repeated stories of orgies involving numerous Pawnee employees were frequently reported. It is not sexual harassment if consenting adults participate in sexual adventures, especially where there are no adverse consequences to the employment relationship.

The plant manager of the Pawnee Products plant in Wichita, KS, was accused of groping the dispatching clerk. The plant manager looked the part of a dirty old man; he was bald, overweight, overly-friendly and a touchy-feely guy. In fact, he was just the opposite of a dirty old man. The complainant was a thirty-one-year old single mother, whose marriage was disintegrating and who enjoyed being part of the fun, instigating numerous instances of sexual banter in which she was an active leader and willing participant. The allegations were serious. I was dispatched from Tulsa to Wichita to investigate. Upon entering the complainant's former office, I found a large sign posted at her desk. The sign read: "Sexual harassment will not be reported... It will be graded." Extensive investigation and the negative results of a lie detector test confirmed that the allegations were simply not true.

The complaining former employee made these charges three days after she resigned her employment when urged to do so by her new husband, who became extremely jealous when she repeatedly came home late from beer drinking sessions after work on Thursdays and Fridays. It is easy to make sexual harassment charges. It is much more difficult to defend them, particularly when most often these charges involve questions of credibility in a he-says,she-says dilemma.

Thrifty Sale to Chrysler

Shortly after my departure from Hall Estill, Thrifty consummated an initial public offering and completed the financing of its annual vehicle fleet through Chrysler Corporation. As a result, Thrifty became a major player in the national car rental industry. In the process, Thrifty changed its corporate image, by adopting new colors, new logos and a new strategic approach, utilizing new Chrysler vehicles where possible. The corporate image involved the word Thrifty slanted to appear modern and the use of soft blue and soft gray colors. The colors themselves became a significant identifying mark in the car rental business, rather than the red and blue rectangle in the past: Red indicated Avis, yellow indicated Hertz, green indicated National and blue now indicated Thrifty. Each of the major national car rental companies had significant and close ties to one of the major automobile manufacturers.

Each car rental company had significant annual demand for new cars. Thrifty was the only major company without any significant tie to a major automobile manufacturer before the Chrysler deal. Simultaneously with Thrifty's growth came the re-emergence of Chrysler Corporation. After negotiating a major $1 billion bail out by the United States government, Lee Iacocca led Chrysler into a new era of growth and significant profitability. Thrifty was a part of that strategy.

Kathy Frame had become the general counsel of Thrifty. Kathy is a terrific lawyer, having served as general counsel of Sonic in Oklahoma City prior to coming to Tulsa. Kathy and I became good friends, even though Hall Estill continued to represent Thrifty in litigation matters. I was extremely pleased that Kathy called me one Thursday afternoon, indicating that the independent members of the board of directors of Thrifty required separate representation in connection with a proposed transaction. I was one of three lawyers offered the opportunity to make a presentation to the outside directors, and fortunately I got the business.

From Friday until Sunday, I worked closely with Kathy, putting together the due diligence documents and files necessary to permit the board to make an informed decision with respect to a proposed friendly tender offer from Chrysler. The outside directors were unfamiliar with the rules governing their obligations when faced with the proposed offer. On Monday, the outside directors and I met with investment bankers for Thrifty and New York counsel to consider a proposed $240 million tender offer. Chrysler's annual shareholder meeting was scheduled for Thursday, and Chrysler desired to make an announcement at its shareholder's meeting that Thrifty had agreed to a proposed acquisition offer.

Outside directors have a legal duty to obtain the advice of an investment banking firm as to whether the offer under the circumstances was fair. Chrysler's offer was significantly above market value for Thrifty's stock, but that alone was insufficient to justify approval of the offer, without independent advice and without the board having gone through the exercise of analyzing the offer against existing marketing and other conditions. By 8:30 p.m. Tuesday evening, the investment bankers had not completed their evaluation. At 11:30 p.m. Tuesday evening, the general counsel for Chrysler called me in my hotel room and advised me that because of the delays during the last three days and because of the board's procrastination with respect to Chrysler's offer, Chrysler decided to preempt that course of action and increase the offer by $37 million. Shortly after that phone call, I was informed by Kathy Frame that the Thrifty board had accepted the increased offer by Chrysler.

The Chrysler general counsel knew the rules and understood the caution and care with which I was advising the outside directors of Thrifty. He also knew that the ultimate exposure was Chrysler's, not Thrifty's. While he concurred in my advice and cautious approach, his client gave him no tolerance for delays. Consequently, to minimize the risk of any shareholder complaint and to expedite approval by the Thrifty board, Chrysler decided to increase its offer. He told me that my thorough and cautious approach was the key factor in Chrysler's decision to raise its offer by more than $37 million. Kathy Frame, Bill Lobeck and Jim Phillion, along with other directors of Thrifty, were ecstatic. Thrifty ultimately accepted a $267 million cash tender from Chrysler. As a footnote, Kathy Frame later married Bill Lobeck, and together they acquired a major interest in National Car Rental. Kathy later was elected Mayor of Tulsa, where she did a terrific job for the people of Tulsa, and she served with distinction the state of Oklahoma in various important capacities.

John Zink Company

While at Baker Hoster, I enjoyed the opportunity to work on several matters with Bob Schwartz of John Zink Company. John Zink was a major manufacturer of burners used in refineries and other heavy equipment used in the petrochemical business. This business involved submission of bids for mechanical, engineering, manufacturing and construction of heavy equipment. One of those disputes involved a project in which Zink was to provide services in refurbishing Ellis Island and the Statue of Liberty. Another involved a major construction project in which claims for product liability issues exceeded $25 million. These issues were successfully resolved by negotiation, not litigation.

Two Zink projects involved environmental remediation and compliance issues. John Zink had shipped one truckload of waste, consisting of approximately 3,200 gallons of industrial solvents, and paint thinner to the Royal Hartage disposal site south of Oklahoma City. The Royal Hartage dumpsite consisted of approximately sixty acres and was the only facility in Oklahoma licensed by the EPA to receive this waste. The Royal Hartage site became one of the top ten worst SuperFund sites and a sludge pit for the major oil and gas companies' disposal of petrochemical wastes. Over a period of several years, the estimated cost to clean up of the Royal Hartage site ranged from the $80 million to $522 million. Zink was one of 500 named potentially responsible parties in the clean up litigation, and it was one of approximately 300 de minimis potentially responsible parties. Zink finally entered into a settlement that provided for the payment of a few thousand dollars in damages.

A more direct EPA problem centered on Zink's clean up efforts at a Kaiser Steel plant near Pryor, Oklahoma, which allegedly was responsible for contaminating ground waters near Grand Lake. Because of an extensive environmental compliance program for its manufacturing products and because of its extensive expertise in burner technology, Zink sought to expand its business into remediation of contaminated sites, through burning soil and through remediation and re-vegetation of grounds near PCB spills. Unfortunately, Zink won the bid to remediate the Kaiser site for $500,000. After spending approximately $1.5 million, the remediation efforts bogged down. I was able to negotiate a resolution satisfactory to the federal district court and the EPA fixed Zink's liability and that completed that project. A poorly drafted proposal, a poorly drafted remediation service contract and extensive uncertainty as to the scope and magnitude of the remediation project led to a fuzzy, unclear scope of work and extensive potential liability for Zink's failure to perform.

In addition to its burner technology, Zink also had a heating, ventilation and air conditioning division that manufactured HVAC equipment for installation on the roof of commercial buildings. A group of managers in this operating division proposed to purchase the assets of the HVAC division, operate those assets on Zink's plant site for three months after closing and continue to use Zink personnel during the transition period. This transaction involved the purchase of substantially all of the assets of the HVAC division, including inventory and accounts receivable, the assumption of only specified liabilities relating to that division and the termination or reassignment of significant numbers of Zink employees who spent part of their time working on HVAC projects and part of their time working on Zink's environmental projects. Allocation of the costs of this arrangement and resolving warranty issues were the only disputed substantive issues in the entire asset purchase transaction.

The transaction was also complicated, because the managers of Zink were becoming owners and operators of the new entity, AAON, Inc. I drafted the letter of intent, the asset purchase agreement and all of the closing documents. John Johnson, then of Gable & Gotwals, represented AAON. This very complicated asset purchase agreement was negotiated in less than two hours. The only significant issue separating the parties dealt with how to allocate liability for warranty claims for work in process and future warranty claims on work completed prior to the closing. This transaction illustrates that a purchase and sale of a business, even one involving more than $10 million, can be completed expeditiously and efficiently if the lawyers and the clients cooperate reasonably in the process.

The Renberg Case

Renberg's had been a permanent fixture in the fine clothing business in Tulsa for more than fifty years. It enjoyed a reputation of excellence in quality and customer service. The store was organized by George Renberg, who had three children; Robert, Don and Sherry. Robert was a high school friend of mine at Edison High School and was married to Nancy. Robert and Nancy and their three children were friends of ours through Holland Hall. Elisa was Laura's tennis doubles partner in middle school, and Devan, their son, played baseball with Kipp on a team I coached. Sherry was married to a lawyer and lived in Kansas City. The Renberg family dispute is a classic example of how good tax planning without an eye toward business control can destroy the golden egg.

For estate planning and tax purchases, George divided the stock, 40% to Bob, 40% to Don, 19% to Sherry and 1% to George. George worked actively in the business despite being more than 80 years old. Each of the Renberg children further divided their stock among their spouses and children for tax and estate planning purposes. This ownership structure set up an inevitable fight between Bob and Don if they ever disagreed, in which Sherry was the tiebreaker, even though she was the Renberg child least associated with the stores.

It was a family tradition that an annual stockholders' meeting would be held with the entire family present. The father, sons and daughter, and their spouses and children were all expected to be there. It was a command performance. The inevitable dispute erupted when Don went to his younger sister and offered to pay her for a proxy to vote her 19% of the shares. She accepted. At the annual shareholders' meeting, Don announced that he held majority control. He fired his older brother, Robert, in the middle of the meeting, with Robert's family watching. He immediately changed the locks on the store doors, filed a garnishment action against Robert for payment of his store account (each of the children had liberal access to charge clothing to a family account), and he refused to allow Robert or Nancy to enter the store.

After more than two years, Bob was unable to obtain any information about the company or its business, was denied payment of a salary or other compensation and was left to seek recourse through litigation. Don refused to pay his sister the next year for her proxy, so she went to Bob to see if he would. Because he had no money, he was unable to do so. A year later, Bob made a proposal to purchase 11% of Sherry's stock, the consummation of which would clearly resolve the control issue and give Robert's family permanent control over the business.

Five days before the annual shareholders' meeting, Robert commenced serious negotiations with Sherry. These negotiations went on through the night and resulted in an agreement pursuant to which Bob would purchase 11% of the outstanding stock held by Sherry, Sherry would give Robert an irrevocable proxy to vote the balance of the 8% held by Sherry and her family, and Sherry would settle her claims that George, Don and Robert were paid excessive annual compensation, thereby depriving Sherry of her fair share of dividends. I represented Sherry in this transaction. I drafted and revised all the documents necessary to implement these agreements.

The stock purchase agreement, the irrevocable voting trust, the various corporate resolutions and the settlement agreement were executed, and immediately Robert did to Don what Don had done to him, against my strong recommendations to the contrary. Don was fired, and Robert elected himself president of the company.

Litigation ensued. George and Don filed suit against Robert and Sherry, seeking to enjoin the closing of this transaction. After filing this litigation but before the closing of the stock purchase took place, Sherry requested that I explain to her how the formula purchase price would be calculated, based upon a specific set of numbers. I drafted a letter to Sherry with these calculations.

At the end of the letter, I urged the parties to close this transaction at the earliest possible time and stated that, "even a judge cannot undo what the parties have consummated." The letter was written to Sherry, marked "attorney-client privilege" and sent in draft form by fax to Sherry's litigation counsel, Jim Sturdevant. Unfortunately, the fax number for Gable Gotwals where Jim worked, and the fax number for Doerner Stuart, counsel representing George and Don, was exactly the same except for one digit. My secretary inadvertently sent the fax to counsel for the opposing parties, and they immediately took it to Judge Scott, requesting an injunction against the closing. Judge Scott simply responded that the comments in my letter were accurate and that he had no power to undo what the parties had in fact consummated. He refused to take any action, which disrupted the closing.

In the middle of this family fight, Devan, Robert's youngest son, completed his Bar Mitzvah requirements. The Renberg family had for more than four generations been major members of Temple Israel in Tulsa. The family was now split apart by aggressive tax planning that gave no thought to control issues. Devan's grandfather was not invited to the Bar Mitzvah. How sad! Claudia, Kipp and I were, and we did attend. The service was awesome. I was really proud of Devan.

My deposition was taken in this case in anticipation of trial over the validity of the stock purchase agreement and the settlement agreement. At trial, I was qualified as an expert witness in corporate matters. I also testified as a fact witness in this case. Sadly, the family dispute played out in court for the world to watch. Millions of dollars in attorney's fees were spent in the litigation of this case.

It was argued that the settlement agreement was simply a device by which Bob would have the company pay for stock he was acquiring from his sister Sherry. The settlement agreement between Bob and Sherry was approved by the court. The end result is that Renberg's has closed its stores, even its base store in Utica Square, and has ceased operating. Robert and Nancy divorced. Don has converted from Judaism to Christianity and attends First United Methodist Church in Tulsa, but the larger family remains very seriously dysfunctional.

Leaving Baker Hoster

During my six years at Baker Hoster, we had monthly partners' meetings, accurate financial reports and full disclosure. I thought we had a strong personal friendship also. I was wrong. We prospered as a firm. The partners had no significant disagreements, at least none that I knew of. Only three issues of any consequence arose during that six-year period in which the partners even remotely disagreed.

Nevertheless, on June 30, 1986, Gary Baker and Gary Clark came to my office and asked me to leave the firm. When I asked why, they refused to answer. They simply said that they were not going to talk about it. To this date, I have never been told why that action was taken. I am still mystified by what took place. For most of the six years I was a partner at Baker Hoster, I led the firm in gross production. I brought to the firm more new clients than any other partner, and much of the new work benefited other members of the firm. I was a team player, but that apparently was not good enough.

I filled a void that no one else in the firm filled, and the firm prospered while I was there. It bothers me still that my partners and my friends would take a precipitous action, without an explanation and without a discussion with me. I never wanted to be a part of a group where I was not wanted or appreciated. At the time, I wondered where my angels were, but they were there. God's plan was in tact. I just did not know it then.

While at Baker Hoster, Laura and Kipp continued to grow and mature. Laura's ninth grade year was spent at the Nick Bollitieri Tennis Academy in Bradenton, FL. When she returned, she played competitive tennis, leading her to a top 2a ranking in Oklahoma in the Girls 18 and to her all-city selection as a senior. In addition, Laura was elected president of her senior class and editor-in-chief of Holland Hall's yearbook. Her graduation from Holland Hall was a major highlight in my life, as well as hers.

Kipp continued to improve in baseball and basketball, where he enjoyed many successes and honors and provided me tremendous joy and excitement. Watching and coaching Kipp in baseball and basketball was as much fun for me as it was for him.

Claudia continued to play her violin professionally with the Oklahoma Sinfonia. She enjoyed playing in the Nutcracker and in other ballets with the Tulsa Ballet and spent most of her time driving the kids back and forth to Holland Hall and taking care of the kids. She did a great job as their mother.

Sole Practice
July 1992-August 1993

Federal Judge Application

On July 1, 1992, I moved into the offices of Craig Blackstock, where I enjoyed an office sharing arrangement for the next sixteen months. Ten days after my departure from Baker Hoster, Judge Cook, the senior federal district trial judge in Tulsa, announced his decision to take senior status. That opened a position on the federal bench. Since before my law school days, I had always thought that one day I would be a federal trial judge. My initial inclinations were confirmed and fostered by my trial experience in the military and by my opportunities to serve as a military judge in special court-martial cases.

Becoming a federal judge, however, requires the recommendation of the senior United States Senator from Oklahoma, the nomination by the President of the United States, successful completion of confirmation hearings before the Senate Judiciary Committee and confirmation by the full Senate. I had no close personal ties to Senator Nichles, to the President or within state or local political movers and shakers. Nevertheless, I viewed the announcement by Judge Cook as an omen and an explanation for why my partners at Baker Hoster decided that my services there were no longer needed.

Before taking any official action to submit my name for nomination, I contacted Tom Golden, a high school friend and former partner of mine at Hall Estill. In the past, he had been a member of nominating committees for federal judicial nominations submitted by Senator Nickles. My lunch with Tom Golden increased my excitement when he urged me to submit my name for nomination.

I also contacted the Hon. Joe Morris, a senior litigation partner at Gable & Gotwals. Judge Morris had been associate general counsel at Amerada Petroleum where my father worked. Judge Morris had been a mentor of mine throughout law school. Every paper I wrote for publication I submitted to Joe for comments in advance of publication. He was always gracious, responsive and encouraging. After leaving Amerada, Judge Morris became dean of the University of Tulsa Law School before his nomination and confirmation as a federal district judge for the Eastern District of Oklahoma. After serving for five years in that capacity, he became Executive Vice President and General Counsel of Shell Oil in Houston. He had worked for Shell early in his legal career. When I disclosed my interest in submitting my name for nomination, Judge Morris' eyes lit up. He told me that his service as a federal district judge was the most exciting and most intellectually challenging time of his life. He urged me to submit my name.

I also contacted several leading lawyers and prominent business persons in Tulsa. I was encouraged at every turn. One of those business leaders was Jim Barnes, Chairman of Mapco. I served with Jim Barnes on the Executive Committee at First United Methodist Church. Others on that executive committee were David Hentchel, Chairman of Occidental Petroleum, and Bob Parker, Sr., Chairman of Parker Drilling Company. Before agreeing to recommend my nomination as a federal district judge, Jim Barnes asked that I have lunch with him. For almost three hours, he quizzed me on a variety of subjects. At the end of that delightful time, he agreed to support my nomination.

Tom Golden later became Chairman of the nominating committee, and Judge Morris was selected as one of the eleven members of that committee. Despite this preliminary work, despite the content of my application, despite the strong recommendations of prominent lawyers and business leaders in Tulsa, despite an effective interview with the nominating committee, I was not selected as one of the three persons whose name was submitted to Senator Nickles for consideration.

I was absolutely convinced that the chain of events leading up to the submission of my application for nomination as a federal district judge was God-orchestrated and God-ordained. When I did not even make the short list, I felt that I had let God down. I became despondent, discouraged and extremely depressed. As it turned out, the name of the person nominated to fill Judge Cook's position on the federal bench in Tulsa and who received President Bush's nomination was never even submitted to the Senate Judicial Committee. Over 120 judicial nominations were suspended, pending the results of the 1992 elections. My angels were there, but I did not see or feel them then.

Depression

A number of other events at work and at home combined to add to my discouragement and depression. My deposition was taken in the Renberg litigation, where various charges and counter charges were made. I was qualified as an expert in corporate law matters in the Renberg trial, and my testimony was a key factor in confirming the legal accuracy of the advice given, the propriety of the settlement reached and the consummation of the stock purchase arrangements made by Bob Renberg, when he purchased his sister Sherry Renberg's stock in the company.

Turbulence and uncertainty within Pawnee Industries was also running rampant. Its failure to meet debt service obligations on the $25 million in loans made to complete the Grand Prairie acquisition, significant quality problems arising because of Dow Chemical's change in the formulation of the principal raw material used in making plastic spas and other leading products caused significant operating losses, resulting in the removal of Brian Klump as chairman.

Brian and Larry Widmer were clients but were also close friends, yet I was asked as counsel to Pawnee to negotiate on behalf of the company their severance arrangements. They felt betrayed by me, though my friendship for them and my representation of the company were ultimately key ingredients in reaching amicable resolutions that were in the best interests of both. Those conclusions, however, were not apparent at the time, at least to them.

A Vision from God

I remember vividly one trip to Wichita, KS, in which I was asked by the board to terminate Larry Widmer's employment. My task was to persuade him that his departure was in his best interest and in the best interest of the company. This meeting followed by several months the termination of Brian Klump, who continued to feel hurt and betrayed by both the company and by me.

As I drove from Tulsa on Interstate 35 east of Perry, OK, clouds boiled, the winds blew and the weather became extremely threatening. I was alone in my car listening to the *Phantom of the Opera* when a vision appeared on the horizon. Very distinctly and very vividly, three crosses appeared out of the clouds with a very bright light showing behind the cross in the middle. I heard without question a voice saying, "Peace be with you. My peace I give to you." That vision marked the beginning of a feeling of peace and comfort over the internal turbulence at Pawnee, over the feelings of betrayal by Larry Widmer and Brian Klump, over my feelings of betrayal by my friends and partners at Baker Hoster, over my feelings of rejection in not being nominated to the federal bench when all the signs pointed clearly to my nomination and over other troubling events occurring in my life. The uncertainty and anxiety I felt did not immediately subside as the clouds disbursed over a five or six minute period. Nevertheless, I mark that point in time as the beginning of a new relationship between me and God.

Sneed Lang
September 1993-January 1996

Starting in September 1993, I accepted a position as a shareholder at Sneed Lang Adams & Barnett. I was encouraged to accept this position by Ray Patton, the former state securities administrator in Oklahoma and soon to be a good friend and partner. Ed Adams, a friend and excellent lawyer, was also a partner at Sneed Lang, whom I came to admire. He had been president of the Downtown Tulsa Kiwanis Club and the Tulsa Bar Association, among other honors. I also received assurances from Jim Lang, Faith Orlowsky and others that Sneed Lang was overflowing with work and needed someone to assist it in all the corporate work that it had to do.

The truth was that Sneed Lang was about to lose its largest oil and gas client, that it had no backlog in corporate or other matters and that the firm simply wanted me to bring my clients and my book of business to assist that firm in covering its exorbitant operating expenses. The $150,000 annual compensation promised proved to be $135,000, and that did not change for the three years I practiced with Sneed Lang.

North Tulsa Project

I was the principal lawyer in the organization, construction, financing and completion of North Point Shopping Center at Pine and Cincinnati in North Tulsa. State Farm Insurance, our client, had a large customer base in North Tulsa, but no support facilities to serve that customer base. At the same time, Congress concluded that banks and other major lending institutions were denying the extension of credit to persons who lived in areas of significant poverty, such as North Tulsa.

This so-called "redlining" policy resulted in federal legislation that mandated banks, savings and loans and other financial institutions make increased credit available in redlined areas and provided tax incentives and tax credits to do so. State Farm envisioned joining with Bank Four in Tulsa and together building a shopping center/office complex that contained an automobile claims service center of State Farm and a branch bank of Bank Four. The desire was to joint venture this project with Public Service Company of Oklahoma, Oklahoma Natural Gas Company and the mayor's office, so that each would have an office in the complex to facilitate cash payments of insurance, banking and basic utility services, which historically were predominantly paid in cash by low income families. This vision resulted in the construction of North Point in Tulsa.

The land for the North Tulsa project was owned by the Tulsa Development Authority as the result of the condemnation and acquisition of property by that public agency. Numerous proposals had been made over 17 years to construct churches, retail shopping centers, grocery stores and similar facilities, but the land was too small to accommodate a major shopping center and was too large for most non-retail projects. The land was vacant for more than 17 years, pending a viable project. The North Point project became that project.

After extensive public meetings and extensive political efforts behind the scenes, a nonprofit organization was formed and State Farm, using both local architects and its corporate architectural expertise from Illinois, completed the design for a major revitalization project in North Tulsa.

The night before the proposed hearing before the Authority, we learned that representatives from Walmart intended to make an alternative proposal, contemplating a small retail shopping center and Walmart at that location. We worked through the night to make color slides and to polish the presentation to secure approval for our project. The purchase agreement had already been negotiated and executed, after extensive changes and modifications to the master land purchase agreement typically used by the Authority. That negotiation in itself was highly charged politically, and each of the changes made represented a hard fought concession that was difficult at best.

The public meeting was held, and the two proposals were submitted. A large audience from the community appeared. Members of the Authority asked numerous questions, and they sought explanations and responses to a variety of issues. A large team from Walmart appeared to make its presentation. At the conclusion of the Walmart presentation, the chairman of the Authority, virtually without discussion, commented that this historic site had remained vacant for more than 17 years and that he was ready to vote. A vote was taken, and the North Point project was unanimously approved.

Dick Smith

Dick Smith had been a senior vice president at Tempo Enterprises when I first met him. Disputes between Dick and Ed Taylor, chairman of Tempo, erupted into litigation during the $46 million merger of Tempo into TCI. The litigation involved options allegedly granted to Dick by Tempo. I have continued to represent Ed Taylor on a variety of personal matters from time to time.

Several years after Dick left Tempo, he requested that I represent him in connection with a dispute involving his stockbroker and financial advisor who worked for Dean Witter. Mr. Smith alleged that the broker unlawfully and without permission converted over $800,000 of his retirement funds into unauthorized investments. Because Ray Patton, a partner of mine at Sneed Lang, often conducted arbitrations for Dean Witter, Sneed Lang was conflicted out of representing Dick Smith in connection with this dispute. Dick's objective was to have his account restored. I referred the matter to a young lawyer friend, who requested a $50,000 retainer. Mr. Smith returned requesting that I seek a waiver of any conflict that Sneed Lang had with Dean Witter.

I negotiated a waiver and an agreement to toll the statute of limitations with the general counsel of Dean Witter in order to provide sufficient time to seek an amicable resolution of the alleged theft. After less than three months and less than $5,000 in my legal fees and expenses, Mr. Smith's account was fully restored, a settlement agreement was reached with the broker, no litigation was instituted and the matter was resolved by agreement.

Bill Robinson

During my time at Sneed Lang, I became acquainted with Bill Robinson, a stockbroker at Prudential Securities. On a whim, Bill had submitted an offer to the federal government to purchase an Egg Harbor yacht that had been used in illegal importation of drugs into Florida, sunk off the coast of Florida and was retrieved by the federal government. The sport fishing yacht had to be rebuilt from stem to stern. In the process of exploring replacement parts, Bill learned that Egg Harbor Yacht Company was suffering difficult financial woes.

Bill's passion for boating and his skill at fundraising led him to seek an acquisition of Egg Harbor Yacht Company, though he had no funds of his own. In November 1994 I drafted a letter of intent pursuant to which Golden Egg Yachts, Inc., a newly-formed company by Bill Robinson, would acquire substantially all the assets and assume certain liabilities of Egg Harbor. This letter of intent led to a long attorney-client relationship with Bill involving virtually every type of business acquisition transaction.

Bill successfully concluded an acquisition of Egg Harbor two years later. However, three months after the acquisition was completed, the major investors, who took control of the board of directors and became senior officers of Egg Harbor after investing about $2 million in cash, terminated Bill Robinson's employment, leaving Bill with in excess of $120,000 in unpaid legal fees. Less than a year later, Egg Harbor filed for protection under Chapter 11.

Bill was extremely focused but extremely difficult to represent. He was conscientious and he acted in good faith. However, good intentions do not pay my mortgage or other financial obligations. His inability to function without experienced legal counsel, his incredible demands for work product always at the last minute, my determination to be serviceorientated and to meet client demands, and his inability or unwillingness to pay for services rendered caused friction and disrupted the attorney-client relationship between us. Bill's continual financial commitments to me, and his constant failure to meet those commitments, though ultimately satisfied in one way or another, resulted in my resignation from the account. My work for Bill was fascinating, always energizing and often fun, but despite those positive feelings, the relationship ultimately came apart when I became increasingly "used" to serve Bill's personal passions.

Departure from Sneed Lang

Sneed Lang was a boutique law firm with three business strengths: litigation, oil and gas, and business. The oil and gas group consisted of four lawyers with strong backgrounds in the acquisition of interests in oil and gas properties and the financing of those acquisitions. Unfortunately, during my time at Sneed Lang, the oil and gas business was in a slow cycle. Just before my arrival, the firm lost its largest client that had kept three of the four lawyers busy almost all of their time.

The litigation group specialized in the defense of white-collar crime and general commercial litigation but also had a large number of plaintiff's cases taken on a contingent fee basis. This proved to be an unstable balance.

The business practice proved stable and ultimately supported and paid for a large portion of the entire firm's overhead. Several of the eleven lawyers failed to produce an amount equal to their own share of overhead during the three and a half years I was at Sneed Lang. Moreover, the firm incurred substantial debt in the hopes that one or more of the contingent fee cases would produce a big victory.

Despite the fact that my production remained significantly above most in the firm, I did not receive a salary increase or a bonus in three and a half years. Toward the end I was asked to look at the financial statements and make recommendations on how expenses could be cut. That was pretty easy. We had far too many support personnel and far too many lawyers not pulling their own weight. Our offices were nice but excessively expensive. During the last year before my departure, only one lawyer other than me received his monthly compensation on time every month. Despite the obviously excessive expenses, no one in the firm was willing to make any of the cuts in overhead necessary to bring revenues in line with expenses. The situation was financially intolerable.

While at Sneed Lang, several defining moments occurred for Laura and Kipp. Laura went to Carlton College in Minnesota and then returned home to attend the University of Tulsa, where she played on the varsity women's tennis team. During that semester, she was accepted at Notre Dame and later graduated Cum Laude with over a 3.6 grade point average. She also accepted admission to Emory Law School in Atlanta.

Kipp graduated from high school, was elected player of the year on his high school baseball team and first team All Southwest Preparatory Conference, hit his only grand slam home run in the conference semi-finals, and accepted a major baseball scholarship to play at the University of Connecticut. Kipp's baseball team journeyed to Laredo, Texas, on the Mexican border to participate in a 16 year old national world series baseball championship, which included twelve teams from as far away as Vancouver, British Columbia, and New York City, as well as Puerto Rico, North Carolina, Texas and other locations. Kipp and his teammates made some wonderful friends, especially the players from Puerto Rico. Kipp and I had a great time.

This was a trying time for me personally, as I moved out of the house into an apartment in September 1995. In October 1995 I attended my first Promise Keepers event in Dallas, TX. This event was a defining moment for me personally, as well as spiritually. In September 1997, I returned to live with Claudia at our home on 36th Court where we continue to live.

Sole Practice Again
February 1996-April 1998

Bill Nay was my closest friend while I practiced law at Hall Estill. Bill and I continue to have a close personal as well as professional relationship. In 1995, Bill Nay and Matt Livingood, another lawyer from Hall Estill, leased office space in South Tulsa and invited me to join them along with three other lawyers. In February 1996, I agreed to do so. Each of us was responsible for our own billings and collections, and we shared common office expenses. We enjoyed being with each other and practicing law with each other for the next two years.

RodMasters

In early July 1997, Rick Heaton called me late one afternoon and told me that he was purchasing a business the following day. We quickly formed a new Oklahoma corporation and prepared a simple bill of sale and an employment agreement for the seller to become his employee. These events set in motion an opportunity for me to get back into the courthouse. Five months later, the seller's employment was terminated for theft of fishing rod products made by the new company. The seller filed an action in replevin, alleging that RodMasters and Rick Heaton sold assets owned by the seller. These were the same assets purchased and paid for by RodMasters. RodMasters denied the allegations and brought several counter claims.

172

After nine separate hearing dates were cancelled, in February 1998, a day-long hearing on the replevin action gave me an opportunity to cross examine Gary Cameron, his wife and his former partner. At the end of this cross examination, Judge Thornbrugh, the trial judge entered a temporary restraining order prohibiting Gary Cameron from making or selling fishing rods, prohibiting him from using the Cameron name in connection with the sale of fishing rods or reels and denying the plaintiffs replevin.

It was fun to cross-examine adverse witnesses, especially ones that lied without reservation, and it was fun to be successful in an adversarial setting. RodMasters finally posted a bond, so that the TRO went into effect, and subsequent hearings continued to reveal the unscrupulous nature of Gary Cameron. I was never paid for the work I did for RodMasters.

Bill Robinson Again

Bill continued to call me at the last minute and increased his incredible, almost impossible, time and work demands on me. I continued to act as Bill's counsel, believing that Bill would one day be successful, because he was so focused, determined, committed and hardworking.

In April 1997, Bill's employment was terminated by Egg Harbor, even though he had completed the acquisition of that company and arranged financing to support it. He returned to Tulsa and became reacquainted with Gifford Mabie and Rhonda Vincent. I had met Gifford and Rhonda three years earlier while I was a lawyer at Sneed Lang. Bill asked me to assist in the completion of a merger of Maxxon, Inc. into a public shell. Maxxon had been formed to acquire the exclusive worldwide rights to manufacture and market a safety syringe that was in development. After completing the merger, I had a continuing opportunity to work with Bill, Gifford and Rhonda on their separate legal matters.

Bill's inability or unwillingness to pay my invoices put incredible strains on my patience and on the professional relationship we had. By early 1998 the receivable from Bill Robinson exceeded $120,000 again and continued to grow monthly. In an effort to resolve this problem, I suggested that Bill pay me in Maxxon stock, even though I did not want to do this. I had never taken stock for a fee in the past. This was contrary to my agreement with Bill, but I needed to resolve this lingering and festering problem.

In late March 1998, I received a call from Gifford stating that he and his group had decided to end their relationship with Bill Robinson. Bill had agreed to devote substantially all of his time and effort in the development of the Maxxon safety syringe and on stockholder relations for Maxxon, but over a period of more than six months, Bill had actually spent virtually all of his time working to get back into the sport fishing yacht business. Maxxon stock had plummeted from almost $5 a share to approximately $0.50 a share, with no reasonable prospects for improvement at the time.

Bill's method of operation and his "lone ranger" style placed enormous and insurmountable difficulties upon his relationship with other members of Gifford's team. Bill returned from a California trip the following Tuesday to learn that his things had been moved out of the Maxxon office and that his relationship was terminated. I acted as a go-between and facilitator to help resolve this employment termination arrangement, so that the disrupted relationship might enable the parties to reach a mutually acceptable and amicable settlement. I was able to successfully conclude an amicable if uneasy settlement.

About a week later, Gifford called me and indicated that he had a vacant office in Maxxon's suite of offices, and he invited me to join with Gifford, Rhonda and Vicki Pippin in their efforts to commercialize emerging technologies. Bill Nay was negotiating an extension of his lease, but each of the other lawyers in the group had encountered opportunities to pursue other professional relationships.

Practicing with Bill Nay had been the high point of my professional career, Nevertheless, the potential offered by Gifford and Rhonda gave me a chance to reduce rather than substantially increase operating overhead, and the opportunity to surround myself with happy, joyous and excited people. My decision to join Gifford and Rhonda hurt Bill's feelings, but thankfully only temporarily. We continue to remain good friends.

While I practiced with Bill Nay, several exciting things happened outside of work. Laura completed law school; she and Claudia traveled together in Ireland; and Laura met Luke Mayes, her future husband. They are so compatible and so happy it thrills me to know of their excitement and their love for each other.

Kipp entered Boston College and was bitten by the marathon bug. The summer between his sophomore and junior years in college, Kipp returned to Tulsa and announced that he intended to run in the marathon. Before returning to Boston College, however, Kipp spent eight weeks in Alaska, hiking on glaciers 450 miles north of Fairbanks, Alaska, and canoeing and kayaking back to Fairbanks. The Alaska trip was a life changing experience for Kipp.

On April 19, 1998, Kipp did successfully complete the Boston Marathon, after having raised more than $1,500 for his charity, the Massachusetts Association for the Blind. After that experience, Kipp came to believe that all things were possible for him. Less than a month after his marathon experience, Kipp was invited to be an intern in the White House in Washington, DC. Kipp also was accepted into the semester abroad program in Quito, Ecuador.

One of the highlights for me came when 497 Promise Keepers from Tulsa went to Washington, DC, for the Stand in the Gap gathering on October 4, 1997. More than 2 million men from all over the world gathered for a time of prayer, repentance, praise and recommitment. I negotiated the lease of the 727 that we chartered for the 497 men who attended from Tulsa and assisted in other efforts to organize and celebrate that event.

1999-2011

The original text of *Angels All Around* was completed in May 1999 as a graduation present for my daughter, Laura, upon her graduation from Emory Law School, and for my son, Kipp, upon his undergraduate graduation from Boston College. The goal was to inform my children about my background and about what I did as a lawyer, so that they would better know and understand me. Thirteen years have passed since that time, and my angels have been hard at work. I have added this post-script to highlight some important events in which my angels have covered me with protection.

The LG Group

In 1998, I joined Gifford Mabie, Rhonda Vincent and Vicki Pippin to form the LG Group, which stands for a "loosey goosey group." Dr. Thomas Coughlin, a heart transplant and thoracic surgeon, later joined the Group as medical advisor. The mission of the LG Group was to acquire and commercialize state of the art technologies. The LG Group formed a new acquisition company, issued blocks of stock to the founders and raised funds to purchase or obtain an exclusive license to practice the US Patent and related intellectual property rights of the target technology. The acquisition company then filed papers with the SEC to enable the acquisition company's stock to be publicly traded in the over-the-counter market.

Before I joined the group, Maxxon, Inc. had already been formed and was publicly traded. I acted as Maxxon's lawyer in certain transactions but I was not an officer or member of the board. Maxxon acquired a technology involving a safety syringe using a vacuum to retract the needle after use. The objective was to prevent accidental needle sticks, a difficult problem for nurses and other health care personnel, sometimes leading to death.

The LG Group identified four technologies that fit its acquisition criteria:

1. Lexon, Inc. acquired a US Patent covering a blood screening test for colon and ovarian cancer.

2. Image Analysis, Inc. acquired a software program that converted grey magnetic resonance images into color images for better clarity.

3. Centrex, Inc. acquired a technology that enabled real time ecoli detection on food products for disease prevention.

4. Nubar, Inc. acquired a laminated carbon fiber reinforcing technology that created a stronger and lighter rebar for heavy construction projects.

In February 2000, I left the LG Group shortly after the stock of Lexon, which had been trading for around $1 a share for more than six months, then suddenly and without explanation or substantive reason, rose to $5 a share in less than three weeks. This dramatic market price rise followed a meeting with a potential investor, who was willing to invest in Lexon if the Lexon stock was trading for $2 a share or more. That investor never did invest in Lexon to my knowledge. The LG Group principals could not explain to me the immediate rise in the market price for Lexon stock, except to say that "the trend is your friend," and "follow the trend, and enjoy the ride." The circumstances made me very nervous.

Many people made a lot of money during this period, but I did not sell my Lexon stock for more than three weeks. I had no inside information. I simply did not know why the stock price went up, and I could not explain the rise from a substantive point of view. I had no evidence of misconduct by anyone at the LG Group, but the sharp and unprecedented rise in the price of Lexon stock caused me to leave the Group. My angels were hovering over me, insuring that I acted honestly and properly under the circumstances.

My association with the LG Group through my departure was very positive. The principals were friends of mine. We had common goals and common interests. My family and I were able to pay for Laura's wedding, pay off many student loans, create an oasis in our backyard with Claudia's wonder garden, and enjoy other benefits as a result of owning stock in the LG Group companies. I learned a great deal and enjoyed the work, for which I will forever be grateful.

LG Group Litigation

In March 2000, less than two months after I left the LG Group, the individual members of the LG Group filed suit against me personally in Tulsa District Court, alleging unspecified negligence. I answered by filing several counterclaims. In March 2000, the LG Group filed another civil action against me, this time in Augusta, Georgia. They obtained a temporary restraining order against me without prior notice to me, preventing me from selling Centrex stock, which I owned as a result of being one of the company's founders. The TRO was immediately dismissed as having no factual basis and as beyond the court's jurisdiction when I answered the allegations.

The LG Group litigation in Tulsa lasted for more than four years, but the betrayal by my friends has lasted much longer. During that time, the LG Group refused to comply with discovery requests and failed to identify or produce any documents to support the frivolous charge that I was negligent in any of the work I did for the Group.

The lawsuit was finally settled when the LG Group bought some of the stock in the LG Group companies which I had given to Laura and Kipp. The settlement occurred a couple months before the civil trial of the *Securities and Exchange Commission v. Gifford Mabie and Thomas Coughlin.*

SEC alleged that Gifford Mabie and Thomas Coughlin engaged in a pump-and-dump scheme involving Maxxon stock and made false and misleading statements concerning Maxxon in violation of federal securities law. I testified as a government witness, after the trial judge held that my testimony was not covered by the attorney-client privilege, which the court ruled had been waived. The jury rendered a $1 million judgment against Gifford Mabie but declined to hold Dr. Coughlin responsible for any of the misconduct. Rhonda Vincent entered into a consent decree and settlement before the trial in which she paid money to settle claims that various SEC filings and financial statements of Maxxon which she prepared were false and misleading.

My angels continued to hover over me during this time. While I was not an officer or director of Maxxon, I had provided legal advice on certain Maxxon matters. The only Maxxon stock that I owned was paid to me in settlement of a past due legal bill owed by Bill Robinson.

Keystone Gas Corporation

In 2000, I did the legal work to form Keystone Gas Corporation and to assist it to acquire the Keystone Gas Gathering System in Creek County, OK. The seller, Duke Energy, financed this asset purchase. Duke had threatened to shut the gathering system down because of environmental and other operating problems. Had that occurred, more than 1,000 small land owners in and around Drumright, OK, would have had no way to market the small amount of gas produced from hundreds of shallow stripper wells.

Over the next several years, Keystone also purchased several other small gathering systems adjacent to and near the Keystone system. In the process, Duke Energy, the original seller to Keystone, sold assets to Scissortail Energy, which Keystone argued were previously sold to it by Duke. The Scissortail litigation and subsequent settlement after more than two years of negotiations consolidated the Keystone system and clarified its very murky title. Subsequent litigation with SemCrude and its successor, Blue Knight Energy, has further clarified Keystone's title to the pipelines and rights of way in the Keystone area of interest.

Powder River Petroleum

Powder River was a Colorado corporation with its principal offices in Calgary, Alberta, Canada. The principal shareholder, who was also the sole director and officer most of its life, was Brian Fox, a citizen of Canada. Powder River's stock was traded publicly in the over-the-counter market. I acted as corporate counsel on certain limited corporate issues referred to me from time to time. My role as a lawyer was limited to general corporate law issues and the settlement of disputes, most of which arose prior to the acquisition of control of Powder River by Brian Fox. My angels protected me from acting as securities counsel for Powder River.

Powder River sold its stock and later sold fractional interests in oil and gas properties to investors in the Far East. The sales were made through an independent oil and gas investment firm in Singapore. Powder River promised a specific rate of return, along with the sale of a fractional interest in oil and gas properties in Texas and Oklahoma. Powder River did not register with state securities authorities in making these sales and did not have a source of funds other than a proposed loan that was never funded to met its commitments to its investors. These transactions resulted in an SEC investigation and state receivership. I did not act as counsel or participate in any of these transactions.

I produced all my records to the receiver appointed to manage Power River, as required by the court and by applicable ethical rules. I also testified for two days during the SEC's investigation of Powder River. Initially, the SEC targeted me individually as a possible defendant, until the SEC staff learned that I did not act as securities counsel for Powder River and I did not participate in the questioned transactions. The SEC ceased any investigation of me shortly after the Tulsa County Bar Association presented me with the Neil Bogan Award for Professionalism. My angels were working overtime during this period of time.

Franchising

From time to time since 1973, I have represented various clients engaged in franchising. During 1999-2011, I acted as counsel for the following start-up franchises: Just Between Friends, a children's consignment sale franchisor; Seeking Sitters, a babysitting franchise; Cookie Advantage, a franchise in which chocolate chip cookies are used to say thank you; Fit for Her, a women's only health and fitness center; and Duraban, a New Zealand company offering various antimicrobial products through local and regional franchises. I provided legal advice to various franchisees, including Camille's, Sonic, The Grounds Guy, Huntington Learning Center, CRP Cell Phone Repair Service, among many others. The infinite variety of businesses that can engage in franchising is staggering, and the legal work associated with those businesses can be very interesting.

Mediation

I attended a week-long seminar in Dallas by the American Arbitration Association about mediation and learned a new way to resolve disputes. This class taught me how to bargain based upon the interests of my client, rather than on their positions. This class also taught me the art of seeking solutions to business problems where both sides to the dispute can win. I followed the AAA basic mediation class by attending a seminar at Pepperdine University in Malibu, CA, on mediating the complex case. There I learned that what we perceive may be very different than what the truth is, because of the financial interest we bring to the issue, the passage of time or a host of other considerations. These mediation classes made me acutely aware of the need to listen more carefully to my clients and to the opposition in order to find a solution to a problem in dispute.

Seeking God's Heart

From 1999 through 2012, I wrote three books: *Seeking God's Heart, A Daily Devotional Journey Through the Psalms; A Treasury of Truth and Wisdom,* and *This I Believe.* My angels were clearly present during the writing of these books. Without my angels, there would be no books authored by me.

On April 23, 2012, I learned that I have Kappa single chain multiple myelona. My white blood cells produce protein, which devour bacteria, fungus and other impurities in operating my immune system. The white blood cells of myelona patients produce too many proteins and some are cancerous. The extra proteins act like Pacman, seeking to devour something, but all the impurities are already destroyed. The extra proteins eat bone. I have little holes in my bones all over my body and an impaired immune system. I also have type II diabetes.

I have written the story of my journey with cancer in a book entitled, *This I Believe*. My cancer was discovered early, before it wrapped around my spine. My cancer is not life threatening, unless it is not treated. I have received 30 radiation treatments and 32 chemotherapy treatments. I have had terrific doctors and medical support personnel. I have had very little pain or other side effects. I have received most of my treatments in Tulsa and I have continued to work while those treatments were being administered. I have enjoyed several miracles in the process. The cancer journey has confirmed my beliefs. God's angels have richly blessed me. I know the following:

1. There is a God who is all knowing, all powerful and always present.
2. My God is real, personal, alive and available to me at all times.
3. My God is present with me wherever I go.
4. God's angels surround me, guiding me and protecting me.
5. My God is in control.
6. I can and do trust Him with everything.

Conclusion

My angels became real in many ways, at many different times, in a variety of different circumstances, so many that it is not possible to deny their existence. I am convinced beyond doubt that God's angels have guided my life, especially at very crucial times in my life. When you discover God's angels in your life, you too will discover that you are blessed beyond belief by their presence and by our loving God. To God Be the Glory!

IN HIS PRESENCE

We are standing on holy ground.
And we know there are angels all around.
So let us praise, praise God know.
For we are in His presence on holy ground.

About the Author

Frederick K. Slicker is a business lawyer in Tulsa, Oklahoma. He holds a Bachelor of Arts in Mathematics (BA) from Kansas University (1965), a Juris Doctor with Highest Distinction (JD) from Kansas University Law School and a Master of Laws (LL. M) from Harvard Law School (1973). He has practiced law since 1968, primarily in the areas of mergers and acquisitions, securities compliance, franchise compliance, purchase and sale of businesses, general business transactions, contracts and business organizations.

Mr. Slicker has been selected by his peers for several years as a "Best Lawyer in America" in the areas of corporate law, mergers and acquisitions, and franchise law. He has earned an AV peer rating from Martindale-Hubbell for many years. He has served on the Tulsa County Bar Association Board of Directors and as Chairman of the TCBA Corporate Section (2001-2002); Chairman of the TCBA Professional Responsibility Committee (2005, 2007 and 2009); Chairman of the TCBA Professionalism Committee (2008-2009); and Chairman of the TCBA Alternative Dispute Resolution Committee (2010-2011). Mr. Slicker received the 2010 Neil Bogan Professionalism Award for "outstanding contributions to the legal profession and to the highest ideals of the profession" from the TCBA. He also was recognized by the TCBA President's Award in 2005, 2007, 2009 and 2010.

He is a frequent speaker at continuing legal education programs for other lawyers. and acts as an independent mediator in business and commercial disputes. He received his mediation training through the American Arbitration Association and the Strauss Institute for Dispute Resolution at Pepperdine University. Mr. Slicker was a Captain in the US Army Judge Advocate General Corps from June 1965 through July 1972, focusing primarily on prosecuting or defending criminal charges.

Mr. Slicker has published several law-related articles, including "A Life in the Practice," 75 OK Bar J. 2559 (2004); "Secondary Defendants in Securities Fraud Litigation Rejoice," 65 OK Bar J. 2587 (1994); and "Church Bonds Blue Sky Survey," Commerce Clearing House Blue Sky Reporter, Part II (November 21, 1985). He is also the author of five books, *A Practical Guide to Church Bond Financing (1985), Angels All Around (1999, 2013), Seeking God's Heart: A Devotional Journey through the Psalms (2004), A Treasury of Truth and Wisdom (2007),* and *This I Believe (2012).*

For more information about Mr. Slicker, go to www.slickerlawfirm.com. To contact Fred, call 918-496-9020 or fax 918-496-9024 or email at fred@slickerlawfirm.com.

CPSIA information can be obtained at www.ICGtesting.com
Printed in the USA
LVOW100827300413

331533LV00002B/4/P